Apology and

When I wrote this book all the sites listed were live and available. When you go to some of them you'll find they've disappeared. God only knows where they go. Some will disappear and some will come back an hour later and some will somehow evolve into a site for Korean folk remedies translated into Hungarian. The internet is indeed a mysterious place. My best advice, if this happens, is to simply move on to the next site. There are plenty listed in each category and the ones that are anxious to sell you something will probably be available longer than some looney trying to cure indigestion with grass seeds or a teenager's homesite.

Lots of people are trying to get rich using the internet, me included, and many of the sites listed here are commercial enterprises trying to suck you into $29.95 a month. If these people are successful I suppose their sites will be around for a long while. I've tried to find mostly free sites but these also tend to disappear when the host gets bored with working for nothing. Regardless, while you can find all these sites for yourself (especially if your time is worth 9 cents an hour) I've done lots of the leg work and locating just one or two useful sites will be easily worth more than the ridiculously low price of this book.

That said, the author, publisher and distributors of this book cannot take responsibility for what you find or don't find or what these sites lead you to, even the pornographic stuff that I didn't intend, or what you may buy and then get stuck with or any of the fascinating, frustrating and endless paths of the internet. Hey, it's the internet. What do you want me to do.

Your Health

You know the old saying. "If you have your health you have everything." You start believing this when you're 40 and your back goes out or you get winded on a flight of stairs or you start swallowing antacid pills like M&M's. This section gives you information on your aging body and some ideas for keeping it young. They do work. I may be 40 but I have the body of a 39 year old.

Medical Sites

- **www.healthfinder.gov**
  This site leads to lots of reliable medical sites. It's run by your government and they wouldn't do anything to mislead you.

- **www.nih.gov/health**
  The National Institute of Health with direct links to the specific institute that supports research related to your health concern.

- **www.mayo.edu**
  The famous Mayo Clinic hosts this site and visiting it is a lot better than traveling to Minnesota in February.

- **www.medscape.com**
  A very comprehensive collection of authoritative medical information and education. It may be geared to doctors but by 40 you're probably smart enough to understand it.

- **www.americanheart.org**
  The American Heart Association keeps you informed about your heart as well as nicely asks you for a donation.

- **www.cancer.org**
  The American Cancer Society will bring you up-to-date on all the latest preventive measures you can take.

I don't want you people to think I'm a hypochondriac or anything but these are great medical sites that will explain everything the doctor is too busy to explain. If you'd like your doctor to spend more than 2 minutes explaining things you're going to have to increase your contribution to your health plan by 40%.

Women's Health

I believe every article on health that I come across. "Broccoli Prevents Cancer", I eat it raw twice a day; "Salt Causes Hypertension", there go the potato chips; "Carrots Improve Night Vision", I turn into a rabbit. This leads to problems, of course, when one article extols coffee and the next damns it but I've decided to just go with the latest postmark. The sites listed here give, I hope, the latest "skinny".

www.coloradohealthnet.org

Harder than usual to find the right info, but worth the effort. Point to Site Overview and then click on Women's Center. The Mayo Clinic's Health Center with information on cancer, fitness and appearance, gynecologic conditions, medical tests and procedures, menopause, osteoporosis, prevention and wellness.

content.health.msn.com/focus_topic/her

This women's health resource will answer your questions on emotional wellness, nutrition, illnesses, sexuality, drugs and even more.

www.womens-health.org

The Society for Women's Health Research tries to rectify biases in medical research and has comprehensive links to every problem you hope you never have.

www.womens-health.com

An excellent interactive learning environment that facilitates the exchange of information. Headaches, mental health, menstrual problems, health news and lots more.

www.womenshealth.org

This forum goes into every aspect of women's health, breaking it down into sections on sex, gyn, body, mind, looks, food and many more categories.

www.nytimes.com/specials/women/whome/index.html

The New York Times reports on women's health and this is "the horse's mouth". In addition there are comprehensive guides to many topics of interest to women from osteoporosis to cosmetic surgery to back pain.

www.4woman.org

The National Women's Health Information Center provides a gateway to a vast array of Federal and other women's health information. Again, it's run by your government.

www.wellweb.com/WOMEN/WOMEN.HTM

Detailed information on every problem you pray you'll never have and the ability to chat with other patients about it.

Men's Health

www.aomc.org/HOD2/general/menshealth.html
The Arnot Ogden Medical Center site for men's health and wellness. Super information even if it does scare you to death.

www.healthtouch.com
An index of male health problems. A well written non-technical review of the major diseases that are out to get us.

www.intelihealth.com
This is Johns Hopkins home site of medical information and there is so much here that if you read it all you will probably qualify to practice medicine.

www.malehealthcenter.com
Another great site for all you hypochondriacs out there. It is run by the Men's Health Center in Dallas. Scroll down and see all the things that can go wrong with you.

medic.med.uth.tmc.edu/ptnt/00000391.htm
Information about exercising for your heart, fats and cholesterol, prostate, and cancer screening.

www.healthwatchers.com/hw/default.asp
Mostly they are trying to sell you various potions that cure everything but it's kind of fun.

www.onhealth.com/ch1/index.asp
Just type in a problem or condition and you'll be buried with information.

www.mediconsult.com
The latest information on men's health in an easy chatty format.

www.healthanswers.com
This is one hell of a medical library. Just type in the part you are interested in and let them terrify you.

www.healthy.net/menshealth
A load of information from a list of every medical school to reports on every disease to articles on andropause which is a controversial counterpart to women's menopause.

Okay, we're not invincible any more. We go for an annual physical and watch our diet. We can't bend over quite like we used to. We're sore for 3 days after playing something with 30 year olds that we shouldn't be playing. We find our stomachs are suddenly very choosy about what they will accept, imagine that just maybe our hair is thinning, and have a back that "goes out" more than we do. It's time to start learning something about what makes our bodies tick and what we can expect from them. These sites will do that.

Hair Loss and growth

Until recently there was little other than sticking a rug on your head to handle the balding problem. Then Rogaine came out and was legitimatized by your needing a prescription to get it, and hair regeneration became a serious field. These sites will expose you to lots of options from pills that may really work, to weaving in hair, to stuff you spray on making your scalp black.

www.regrowth.com
A very comprehensive site with all sorts of treatments and remedies from green tea to transplants and an honest evaluation of each.

hometown.aol.com/hairbook/index.htm
Hair Loss Information Center gives a superb background on hair and its characteristics and a detailed analysis of each kind of treatment.

www.propecia.com
Details on Propecia, a prescription drug from Merck which has been found helpful in controlling baldness.

www.hairsource.com
This site sells all sorts of non-prescription hair loss remedies of a kind that used to be recommended by your bald barber.

www.unibio.com
This site sells Natural Cosmeceutuals (whatever that is) and promises amazing hair growth from some pretty expensive stuff. You're old enough to be wary of claims like this.

www.morehair.com
A great deal of very sound information. I wish I had time to read it all because I'm getting a little thin on top.

www.regenhair.com
A lot of promises that go against all the above medically approved advice but even quacks have to earn a living.

www.luxor-of-paris.com/prices.htm
Another herbal remedy "guaranteed" to prevent baldness. From Paris no less.

Women's Medical Concerns

- **www.msnbc.com/news/BRCANCER_Front.asp**
  The latest studies, tests, trends, and prevention.
- **www.fight-breastcancer.com**
  A highly regarded breast cancer resource with survivor stories, myths, state initiatives and a reminder that nothing replaces early detection.
- **www2.cancer.org/bcn/index.html**
  The American Cancer Society's breast cancer network with survivorship, information, resources and news.
- **www.acor.org**
  A free online cancer information site with excellent links to new developments and a very encouraging reconstruction story.
- **www.cancerhelp.com/ed**
  Frequently asked questions on coping and surviving breast cancer from Edu-Care's breast cancer network.
- **www.graylab.ac.uk/cancernet/600062.html**
  National Cancer Institute's site on Inflammatory Breast Cancer.
- **www.breastcancerinfo.com**
  This breast cancer foundation brings you the latest developments and very moving survivor stories.

If you're not worrying about your kids, breast cancer is probably a woman's biggest anxiety. Let's hope you never even have to think about needing these pages other than to learn that smoking increases your risk.

Plastic Surgery

Some women turn 40 and want to do crazy things like change their careers or get huge tattoos. If you are really anxious to reshuffle your life why not just get a boob job.

- **www.surgery.org/procedures/home.html**
  Introduction to cosmetic (only) surgical procedures from the American Society of Aesthetic Plastic Surgery. Detailed information on each type of plastic surgery and a searchable list of surgeons certified by the American Board of Plastic Surgeons.

- **www.plasticsurgery.org/surgery/prcdidx.htm**
  Web Site sponsored by the American Society of Plastic Surgeons and the Plastic Surgery Educational Foundation offering links to all types of reconstructive and cosmetic surgery. You can also find a list of surgeons in your area.

- **www.surgery.com**
  Provides information about cosmetic surgery procedures. Assists in locating a surgeon, reviewing the surgeon's credentials, viewing before and after photographs of the surgeon's work and even e-mailing the surgeon directly. You pick the area you would like to improve, and before and after pictures provide a realistic view of actual improvement from procedures. Links to Plastic Surgeons in your area.

- **www.onlinesurgery.com/live/index.html**
  If you have Real Player, you can watch, on line, any number of plastic surgical procedures. Choose from face lift, liposuction, breast reduction or enhancement, nose job. See post-op interviews. Not for the faint of heart.

- **www.plasticsurgery.org/surgery/dermabra.htm**
  Refinishing the skin, also known as dermabrasion and dermaplaning gives the skin a smoother appearance. It is most often used to smooth out facial wrinkles, treat deep acne scars, or remove pre-cancerous growths.

Back Pain

- **text.nlm.nih.gov/ftrs/tocview**
  The causes and what to do about the plague of lower back pain.
- **www.ninds.nih.gov/patients/Disorder/back%20pain/backpain.htm**
  The National Institution of Health will tell you all about back pain. It probably won't help.
- **www.ama-assn.org/insight/spec_con /patient/pat007.htm**
  The AMA tells you everything about prevention and treatment of back pain.
- **www.aaos.org/wordhtml/pat_educ.htm**
  Orthopaedic surgeons tell you all about your back as well as the rest of your bones and muscles and problems from shoes to carpel tunnel.
- **www.vh.org/Patients/IHB/Ortho/BackPatient/Contents.html**
  This site is published by a non-government panel of experts and has excellent and sound advice on back pain and prevention.
- **www.mayohealth.org/mayo/9402/htm/backcare.htm**
  The Mayo clinic gives you all they know about back pain. Short of seeing an expert in person, this is sound stuff.

Humans just weren't meant to walk around standing erect and the result of leaving the trees and rising to the top of the food chain is back pain. If yours hasn't acted up yet just save this page for a few years.

Skin

The 17 year old complexion is hard to duplicate after 40 years of exposure to sun and wind and "hickies" but these sites may help and will at least convince you to use lots of sun block.

- **www.cdc.gov/chooseyourcover**
  You may still love the sun but after reading this you'll learn to cover up and use lots of sun block.
- **www.aad.org/patient_intro.html**
  Dermatologists will frighten you even more about skin cancer but also give you information on varicose veins and acne (You don't still have acne?).
- **www.mayohealth.org/mayo/library/htm/ tocskinc.htm**
  You can hardly find a better source of advice on every kind of skin condition than this site from the Mayo Clinic.
- **www.nlm.nih.gov/medlineplus/skinhairandnails.html**
  This long site is your government giving you the honest facts on skin, hair and nails. You won't find anti-aging creams and magic bust enlargers here.
- **www.nytimes.com/specials/women/warchive/960619_1213.html**
  Amongst much other information this site will convince you to stop smoking. It seems it causes wrinkles.

Sexuality

- **neuro-www.mgh.harvard.edu/forum_2/EpilepsyF/sexdrive.html**
  The Department of Neurology at Mass. General Hospital maintains this forum on sex drive and they should know what they're talking about.

- **gynpages.com**
  Abortion Clinics online. Just in case, etc.

- **femina.cybergrrl.com/explorer.htm**
  Sites for, by and about women. You can learn all about subjects with which you are too embarrassed to talk to your best friends.

- **www.atfloydian.u-net.com/alt-contraceptives/home.htm**
  An amazingly comprehensive privately run site with information on alternative contraceptives as well as sterilization, sexual health and myths like avoiding pregnancy by jumping up and down after sex.

- **www.askisadora.com/index2.html**
  A sexuality forum that will keep you too busy with the discussions and links to even think of having sex.

- **www.sexologist.org**
  The American Board of Sexology. It seems they actually certify people to be sex therapists. If you need one check their credentials.

- **www.playcouples.com**
  Don't open this one unless you are very liberal minded.

- **www.todayswoman.com**
  This is supposed to be a general women's site with fashions and parenting and such but it seems to be mostly sex so we'll put it here.

You should really be enjoying sex at age 40 and if you're not you are doing something wrong. You can try to figure out your mistakes and expand your sexual horizons on the internet in more ways than looking at the pornographic sites.

Sex Drive

Sex drive is probably more in your head than in your diet so take all the vitamins and sex enhancers that you see on the internet with a grain of salt and then see your psychologist. Find out on this page about the real and the ridiculous.

- **www.mens-page.com**
  This site deals with impotence and male menopause. The stories are frightening and I recommend skipping this site if you have hypochondriac tendencies.

- **www.ama-assn.org/special/contra/support/ppfa/vasecto4.htm**
  By the time you type in this address you'll probably have changed your mind but here is all the intelligence about a vasectomy.

- **www.baaaa.com/adnet/eros3.htm**
  "Put the lead back in your pencil" with Eros Sex Drive Enhancer. Who knows, if you believe it'll work maybe it'll work. I'd rather eat oysters.

- **neuro-www.mgh.harvard.edu/forum_2/EpilepsyF/sexdrive.html**
  The Department of Neurology at Mass. General Hospital maintains this forum on sex drive and they should know what they're talking about.

- **www.med.umich.edu/obgyn/vulva/sandp.html**
  An excellent discussion of women's sexual discomfort and how to cure it.

- **content.health.msn.com/content/dmk/dmk_article_58756**
  A very comprehensive discussion of hormonal and physical sexual changes during pregnancy.

- **www.thriveonline.com/sex/experts/delilah/delilah.topic.html**
  I don't know who "Delilah" is but she sure knows all about every aspect of women's sexuality from flirting to foreplay to fantasies.

Sexually Transmitted Diseases

- **www.mdchoice.com/Pt/PtInfo/std.asp**
  A brief explanation of various sexually transmitted diseases. The search boxes at the top of the site will give you more information than you want.

- **www.mediconsult.com**
  A comprehensive site that gives you information on everything that can go wrong. Just pick a condition that is troubling you and let the doctors fill you with fear.

- **www.condomania.com**
  Avoid trouble next time with one of this company's many styles of condoms. They even rate different brands.

- **www.healthanswers.com**
  Just click on STD and receive expert advice on so many scary diseases that you'll learn to keep your pants zipped or knees together.

- **www.healthlinkusa.com/276feat.htm**
  A very comprehensive site with a wide range of information and links to even more.

At your age you should know better, but in the event there are some funny rashes itching around your body this is the place to find out just what you may have caught. The good news, I suppose, is that you are still pretty sexually active.

Vision Concerns

Sick of your contact lenses or glasses? Been hearing about the new surgical vision correcting procedures? I for one have been interested for years but I've been a coward when it comes to sharp objects or lasers fooling with my eyes. In case you are braver, here is the place to learn more.

- **ophthalmology.about.com**
  An excellent overview on all the new eye surgery techniques. Search under "vision correction" on the bottom and if you read it all you'll qualify for an Ophthalmologist degree.
- **www.asklasikdocs.com**
  Board certified surgeons answer every possible question on Lasik surgery in great detail.
- **www.lasersite.com**
  Laser eye surgery explained and a directory of doctors who perform this surgery.
- **www.ftc.gov/bcp/conline/pubs/health/ vision.htm**
  This government site has an excellent discussion of vision correction procedures. It really helps you to read between the lines of all the sites selling vision correction procedures.
- **encarta.msn.com/find/Concise.asp?ti= 0558A000**
  If you are having vision problems for the first time this is a good site to give you a little background on just what glasses and contact lenses do.

Weight Stuff and Nutrition

- **www.americanheart.org/Whats_News/AHA_News_Releases/obesitytips.html**
  Tips on finding a healthy weight for yourself from the American Heart Association. By the time, of course, that you've typed in this address you'll have lost a pound or two.

- **www.eatright.org/nfs/nfs51.html**
  American Dietetic Assoc. answers questions on nutrition and fitness.

- **www.thriveonline.com/health/Library/CAD/abstract1638.html**
  Fitness, nutrition, sexuality and serenity. What more do you need?

- **www.fitnessmagazine.com**
  Mind, body and spirit for women from Fitness Magazine. Lots of good articles.

- **www.acsh.org/nutrition/index.html**
  The American Council on Fitness and Health will give you articles on every food that will cure or kill you.

It's normal to gain a little weight as you grow older but there comes a time when you have to draw the line in the sand or end up being a fatty. These sites will help you at least establish some bench marks about where you should be and what you should be eating to get there.

Diets

There are millions, maybe billions of diets on the web and in fact anytime your computer is working too slowly you can be sure it's because fat people are looking up more diets. I know you're not one of them but if you do want to lose a little weight here are a few sites that will help you.

- **www.catabolic.com**
  This diet claims to work 3 times faster than starvation. It's based on 100 foods that burn more calories, being digested, than they provide. It costs $19.95 to learn what they are.
- **www.dietinfo.com/diets.htm**
  This site lists a zillion diets, clinics and centers. If you follow each for a day you'll end up weighing nothing.
- **www.dietsite.com**
  A free service that will analyze your diet. They also talk about sport nutrition and alternative nutrition which seems to mean herbs.
- **www.obesity.com**
  A scary web address, Obesity.com (Da-da-da-dum), but there is very well presented information on health and weight loss and yes, a number to tell you if you are obese.
- **www.fatfree.com**
  The fat free and low fat archive with recipes that will make your diet a fun experience.
- **www.diets-and-weight-loss.com/atkins.htm**
  Learn about Dr. Atkin's diet and how you can buy into losing weight.

Diets

- **www.cambridgediet.com**
  With the Cambridge diet you buy and eat a lot of their goo and they promise you'll lose weight.
- **www.weightwatchers.com**
  Weight Watchers must work cause they have meetings all over the world. They offered to find one in your country and I picked a place named EESTI, God only knows where, and sure enough they had a Weight Watchers. What's more the site was in EESTIAN or whatever.
- **www.prevention.com/weight/wlwb**
  You just tell them what you'd like to weigh and they'll tell you just how many calories a day you can eat. The 71 weight loss tips are pretty good.
- **www.nutra-slim.com/mega4.html**
  This site is a scream. The special Accelerated Fat Burning diet lets you "burn up fat" even while you sleep. Mostly you'll just keep clicking on wild claims until you reach the $19.95 plus $4.85 shipping and handling finale.
- **www.oxycise.com**
  With this weight loss program you don't diet or take pills or buy gadgets. You just use oxygen. All you have to do is buy the videos, and breathe, and you'll be skinny in no time.

Some of the diet sites on this page offer serious help. Others offer ridiculous fantasy. Now that you're over 40 I can assume you'll be able to pick out the difference and I'm including the ridiculous ones for your amusement.

The Stuff You Eat and What It Does To You

When you get to be 40 you can no longer eat and drink with abandon. You start to carry antacid pills everywhere and no longer sleep well if you eat bratwurst and cream pies after 9 PM. These sites will give you some idea of what's good for you and not, if you haven't already figured it out.

www.navigator.tufts.edu
This site performs a remarkable service in rating over 200 nutritional web sites based on accuracy, depth of information and usability.

www.mayohealth.org
The Mayo Clinic's Health Oasis has a nutrition center that Tufts rated the highest. You might as well get your nutritional information from the best.

www.pueblo.gsa.gov
According to the Tufts rating your government is on the stick here with an excellent site that gives good information on food and its effect on your health.

vm.cfsan.fda.gov/list.html
A complex and serious site but if you have a particular subject in mind here is where you get real solid advice. Look up, for example, Health Claims On Food.

www.ama-assn.org/consumer.htm
The AMA Health Insight is a very useable site with excellent information on everything you should or shouldn't stick in your stomach. You have to believe them, they're your doctors.

www.cyberdiet.com
A fun site with all the tools you need to plan a healthful diet. Check out the Fast Food Quest and see what you are really eating.

Fitness

- **www.fitnesslink.com**
  A neat site with all sorts of information on exercise, nutrition, and gyms.

- **www.mensfitness.com**
  The site for Men's Fitness magazine which has some pretty good information on training, nutrition, health and gear.

- **www.acefitness.org**
  This site lists 40,000 certified personal trainers. One of them has to be able to inspire you to exercise more.

- **www.primusweb.com/fitnesspartner/library/libindex.htm**
  Excellent equipment and book reviews. Check this out before you spend money.

- **www.pitt.edu/~pahnet**
  The Physical Activity and Health network tells you how beneficial exercise is with basic articles from the leading sources. You've probably heard all this before and just didn't listen.

- **www.vitality.com/vfm.html**
  Vitality Magazine's site with a fair list of tips on health.

- **www.newsdirectory.com/news/magazine/health**
  A directory of about 35 health magazines from the U. S. and U.K., many on specialized subjects like massage and deafness.

More exercise. That's the one thing all the magazines insist will extend your life and you never see an article disputing it 6 months later. So get with it and I hope you'll find a little inspiration from some of these sites.

Vasectomy

The very mention of this word terrifies me but it is hailed as one of the safest and easiest birth control methods. Well, at least until recently, when a few reports have surfaced about it possibly causing some kind of prostate or cancer problems. Check it out before you cut or just wait a few weeks and another study will refute it anyway.

- **www.plannedparenthood.org/BIRTH-CONTROL/allaboutvas.htm**
  Everything about Vasectomies from Planned Parenthood. Who are these "planners"?

- **www.geocities.com/fl_cheshire**
  A vasectomy forum for men to discuss experiences and issues.

- **www.vasectomy.ca**
  This site describes a "no scalpel" vasectomy plus has an excellent discussion of the general advisability of the procedure. Anything that avoids a scalpel is worth looking into.

- **oncolink.upenn.edu/pdq/600326.html**
  This study examines increased risk of prostate cancer after a vasectomy. Something you'll want to investigate.

- **www.gynpages.com/ultimate/vasectomy.html**
  Some good links on this site about the "ultimate birth control" method.

Tattoo Removal

www.patient-info.com/tattoo.htm
An excellent discussion of the different methods of tattoo removal. The laser ones are the only that don't appear to hurt.

www.lasersociety.org
Laser tattoo, scar and wrinkle removal with before and after pictures.

www.removal.webhost.com.au/index1.html
This is a rather complete discussion of one man's tattoo removal experience.

www.undoyourtattoo.com
This clinic explains how removal is done and answers questions.

www.tattoomd.com
A board certified physician explains tattoo removal and shows excellent photos.

www.tattooz.com/tattoo_sites.htm
If all the talk about removal has got you interested in getting a tattoo, this site offers links to some very impressive artists.

At 40 you may be interested in removing some of the indiscretions of youth. Here are places that give information on tattoo removal or, if you've never had a tattoo, perhaps you can try one knowing they're not as permanent as they used to be.

Alcohol

Alcohol can be a real health problem. Too much that is. A little is supposed to be good at least this month. Mostly the people who are having trouble with their drinking won't admit it so this page probably will do little good but perhaps you have a friend....

- **content.health.msn.com/content/article/1674.50182**
  Information when alcohol becomes a problem.
- **www.alcoholics-anonymous.org**
  If you have friends who need help, Alcoholics-Anonymous is the place to send them.
- **www.ncadd.org**
  The National Council on Alcohol and Drug Dependence. Don't let the picture of the founder scare you. There is good information here.
- **alcoholism.miningco.com/health/alcoholism**
  Links to a billion (well maybe a hundred) alcohol-problem related areas.
- **www.health.org**
  A real lot of information from the National Clearinghouse for Alcohol and Drug Information. If you read all of this you'll have no time left to drink.

Compulsive Gambling

- **mayohealth.org/mayo/9712/htm/gambling.htm**
  Help from the experts at the Mayo clinic on this 500 billion dollar a year problem.
- **www.intervention.com/gambling**
  When to intervene with someone who may have a gambling problem.
- **www.ncpgambling.org**
  The National Council on Gambling has 10 questions to ask yourself.
- **www.gamblersanonymous.org**
  Gamblers Anonymous home page.
- **www.slotland.com/?p=334500**
  In case you're not having a gambling problem this site lets you play the slots. Have fun.

Gambling, like drinking, is not something with which you ever see yourself having a problem. View a few of these sites, just for fun, and you may get to know yourself a little better.

Alternative Medicine

If you hate to go to doctors or if you don't trust doctors or if the doctors haven't been able to cure what ails you, there is always alternative medicine to turn to. With alternative medicine you can often get totally untrained quacks and dangerous unsanitary nuts to do ridiculous things to your body. The funny thing is sometimes these treatments work. Who am I to knock them. Some kinds of alternative medicine have even entered mainstream health care. You can read about alternative treatments here and make your own judgments.

homeopathic-md-do.com
This is a national list of real MD's who practice classical homeopathy which as I understand it consists of giving you an extremely diluted form of a poison in an appropriate dose matched to the poison that is making you sick. Or something like that.

www.powerfate.com
This product, for only $39.95, claims to actually makes good luck happen. It works by absorbing all the "negatives" in your life. In case it doesn't work there is a PowerEnhancer for only an additional $9. And a money back guarantee no less. Don't miss this site if you need good luck.

spiritualnetwork.com/links/New
You can click on this site for actual divine insights ($70 per hour) and links to such diverse "medical treatments" as Hemp Oil, Tarot readings, Shazam Astrology, Aumara Light and Healing circles and other things that defy human comprehension.

www.lisco.com/wuebben/TM/health.html
Maharishi Vedic creates heaven on earth with this website of bliss and enlightenment.

Snoring

www.snoring-strips.com

This site sells "chin up breathing strips" which you stick around your jaw and hope no one sees you while you sleep cause you look pretty ridiculous. They swear it helps.

www.snoringless.com

For 20 bucks you spray this stuff in your throat and it lubricates the snoring spot so everything is quiet.

www.snoring-help.com/index.html

This site sounds like real doctors that treat serious snoring with surgery and radio frequency waves as well as snoring help appliances.

hometown.aol.com/roctex69/myhomepage/index.html

Here's a good solution. This site sells some sort of electronic earplug that you give to whomever is complaining about your snoring. Then the whole problem is off your back.

www.snaplab.com/infosn1.htm

Snap Laboratories sends you a recording device to record your snoring which they analyze, if you can believe it, and send to your doctor who then cuts your throat out (just kidding).

Does your mate and even people in the next room complain about your snoring? Does your snoring even wake you up? Well, when that happens it's time to do something about it. These sites all tell you snoring is not a funny problem so don't think this is just a joke.

Mental Health

These are the sites that will let you know if indeed your family is driving you crazy. I've found that by the time you're 40, however crazy or not you may be, you're pretty satisfied with your personality and not too interested in changing it. Perhaps you can use these sites to prove to yourself just how nutty everyone else is.

- **www.mentalhelp.net**
  An award winning online guide to mental health and psychiatry. They even have a mental health store with herbs and stuff to make you better.

- **www.metanoia.org/choose/index.html**
  Sound advice on choosing a mental help therapist in case life just doesn't seem to be working or you are hurting inside.

- **depression.about.com/health/depression**
  An extensive guide to depression and information on causes, defining it, treatment, and much more.

- **www.mentalhealth.com**
  An encyclopedia of mental health information. The most common disorders are listed with descriptions, diagnosis and treatment. Enough links to absolutely everything about the subject to truly drive you crazy.

- **www.mhsource.com/expert**
  This professor of psychiatry at Tufts provides a free service that will answer your e-mail questions.

Recurring Dreams

redrival.com/nightmare/dictionary.html
Your online dream dictionary can help you remember and explain your dreams, if you dare. Most unpleasant dreams seem to have a basis in insecurity.

dreams.nsm.it/dreams/varie/bears.html
Tell this site about your dreams and they will try to interpret them. I'm not so sure I'd want them to.

www.shpm.com/articles/dreams/index.shtml
Self Help and Psychology magazine has some wonderful articles on using dreams to improve your life.

1st-spot.freeservers.com/topic_dreams.html
A great list of sites about dreams. If you start checking these out you'll have no time left for sleeping.

www.lifetreks.com
These people do research into dreams and need your dreams. You can give at the office (if you nap there) and also at home. Fun lists of other people's dreams.

Do you still have that dream about final exams? You know the one where you have to pass this course to graduate and you haven't been to a single class all year. A version that I sometimes have is being unable to find the exam room. Well, join the club and learn about other people who suffer the same way and maybe even learn what to do about it.

Yoga

Rather than running up and down hills or sweating at smelly gyms you can take up yoga. You'll sweat just as smelly but will probably feel spiritually superior to all the other weekend athletes. It'll keep you flexible and if it doesn't actually make you younger it should give you the inner peace to stop worrying about being 40.

- **www.yogasite.com**
  An eclectic collection of yoga connections. It gives the postures and describes a dozen styles that will confuse you no end.
- **www.yogaclass.com**
  A lovely site with a free online yoga class. Here is an easy way to get started with no cost or embarrassment.
- **www.will-harris.com/yoga**
  Yoga exercises you can do at your desk. You'll feel great but your co-workers will think you've lost your marbles.
- **www.santosha.com/asanas/asana.html**
  Instructions on a long list of yoga poses. Pronouncing the names looks as difficult as bending 40 year old bodies into the position.
- **www.sivananda.org**
  This award winning site has 345 pages. If reading them alone would only make you more flexible I'd read it all.

Travel

Look, you're 40. If you don't see the world now, just when are you going to do it? The time to take all those trips you've been dreaming about is while you have your health and the ability to really enjoy them. This section has a bunch of pages that make travel planning and travel arrangements easy. As for the kids, check out page 121, Kids' Camps and Trips, so you can get away by yourself. The following 2 pages list the online sites of most major American and foreign airlines.

U.S. Airline Sites

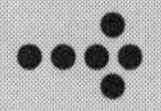

To make reservations, find out schedules and most important get the extra frequent flier miles, book your flight on these sites.

Alaska Airlines	www.alaskaair.com
American Airlines	www.AA.com
Continental Airlines	www.continental.com
Delta Airlines	www.delta-air.com
Northwest Airlines	www.nwa.com
Southwest Airlines	www.southwest.com
TransWorld Airline	www.twa.com
United Airlines	www.ual.com
US Airways	www.usairways.com

Some Foreign Airlines

Air Canada	www.aircanada.ca
Air France	www.airfrance.com
British Airways	www.british-airways.com
KLM Airlines	www.klm.com
Lufthansa	www.lufthansa.com
Swissair	www.swissair.com

Travel Books Online

- www.fodors.com
- www.frommers.com
- www.lonelyplanet.com
- travel.roughguides.com
- www.wtgonline.com/navigate/world.asp
- www.zagat.com

While these sites don't always give you the entire book (let them make a living) you can get an incredible amount of information about virtually every tourist location in the world. It is the smart place to look when you start planning a trip.

Worldwide Health Warnings and Information

If you're going to take a great vacation or trip, the last thing you want is to die from some horrible disease that creeps up from your bare feet and infects your brain with a worm that crawls out your nose or worse. Likewise, most folk would rather not be kidnapped by mustached banditos who cut off ears for ransom. Check out these warning sites before making your non-refundable reservations.

- **www.who.int/emc/outbreak_news**
  Find out about the black plague before you leave.
- **www.cdc.gov/travel**
  Health requirements and medication recommendations for anywhere in the world.
- **travel.state.gov/travel_warnings.html**
  Travel warnings that even the CIA listens to.
- **www.tripprep.com/index.html**
  General trip information, health precautions, disease risk summary, official health data, and US advisories.
- **www.pathfinder.com/travel/TL/links/ health.html**
  Links to multiple health sites. Everything from diving medicine to high altitude sickness.

Travel Clothing

- **www.exofficio.com**
  The ultimate clothing in which to see the world.
- **www.tilley.com**
  This Canadian company has some fun customs you're supposed to carry out when you meet someone else wearing their stuff.
- **www.travelsmith.com**
  I have personally used this company a great deal and have never been sorry.
- **www.fibronet.com.tw/wool/finepacking.html**
  This site tells you how to pack. It's pretty basic stuff but in case you haven't traveled since the kids were born it might be a good review.
- **www.llbeam.com**
  L.L. Bean where not only can you get travel clothes but also the pack to stuff them in.

You don't want to look like a geek when you are representing your country overseas, do you? Better get some of these wrinkle resistant, washable wonders from companies that specialize in travel wear. These clothes will also help you blend in with all the other tourists so the natives won't mistake you for someone with whom their family has a blood feud.

Active Vacations for 40 Year Olds

You've been to Europe, seen the States, recognize the hazards of too much sun on a beach and gained weight on cruises. Perhaps now you're ready for active vacations. These will take you to more remote places and teach you new things that you need to stay alive like Eskimo rolling your kayak, boiling your water, and shaking deadly insects out of your boots. You'll come home needing a week in bed before going back to work.

- **www.gorp.com/akdisc.htm**
  Alaska adventure trips. White water rafting, hiking, canoeing etc.
- **www.belize.com/reef%2Dscuba.html**
  Scuba diving and snorkeling in Belize on their barrier reef.
- **www.goski.com**
  Your ski vacation site.
- **courseguide.golfweb.com**
  This is a good guide to golf courses around the world.
- **www.greatoutdoors.com/index.html**
  Great outdoor activities of all kinds with links to equipment and ratings.
- **www.away.com**
  A travel company that specializes in adventure travel.

Active Vacations for 40 Year Olds

- **www.serendipityadventures.com/rugged.htm**
  Rafting, hiking, climbing, biking and more in Costa Rica.
- **www.fodors.com/sports**
  Over 500 sport and adventure trips in North America from sky diving to covered wagon trips.
- **www.llamatours.com**
  Llama tours in British Columbia. Let the llamas carry your gear.
- **www.beachs%2Dmca.com**
  Spend your vacation seeing the world from the back of a motorcycle.
- **www.outsidemag.com**
  Outside Magazine's site with destinations for active trips around the world.
- **www.spectrav.com**
  Adventure and special interest travel links to the operators of everything from dog sleds to cattle drives.
- **activetravel.about.com**
  A network of sites about all sorts of active trips plus every other kind.

The real key to a great active vacation is finding an outfit that will make you, and everyone you tell about the trip for years to come, think the trip is death defying while keeping you absolutely safe. Hopefully these sites will do that.

Exotic Vacation Travel

Go to wildly exotic spots now. After retirement, your back or knees will probably be gone and you won't enjoy yourself. 40 is a fine time to start seeing all those places you've been dreaming about and here are a few sites to whet your appetite.

www.aandktours.com/html/index.html
Abercrombie and Kent's site. Check out the Marco Polo Club for remote and exotic locations.

www.lonelyplanet.com/dest/dest.htm
Lonely Planet's in depth descriptions of exotic locations.

www.hotwired.com/rough
This is the Rough Guide's site which gives information on exotic locations (14,000 they claim) around the world. The information is very detailed and complete.

www.africaarchipelago.com/home.html
This London agency specializes in travel to East Africa.

www.tourism-asia.com
The insiders guide to travel throughout Asia.

www.virtualnorth.net
Just type in the kind of arctic vacation you want and they will come up with the outfitters. Do they bring portable toilets?

Women's Travel

> Women traveling by themselves or with other women have different concerns and needs. An entire industry has grown up to meet them. Leave the guys at home and enjoy a different kind of totally stress-free vacation.

- **www.rainbowadventures.com**
  Adventure travel for women over 30.
- **www.exploretravel.com/Women.html**
  Outdoor and cultural travel for women over 40.
- **www.journeywoman.com**
  An online travel resource just for women.
- **www.napanet.net/~satchel**
  A new travel magazine for women over 40.
- **maiden-voyages.com**
  An online edition of a women's travel magazine that lists lots of companies specializing in women's travel.
- **maiden-voyages.com/directory/ventures.html**
  Links to companies offering a broad range of trips including adventure, hiking/biking, dude ranches, cultural/theater, culinary.
- **womenstravelclub.com**
  Designed for women by women. Travel to over 20 destinations annually.
- **www.women-traveling.com**
  Women Traveling Together (WTT) offers escorted, all-inclusive tours for women of all ages who want the companionship and security a small group offers, while having the option to participate in planned activities or strike out on their own.
- **travellady.com/special.html**
  From Travellady Magazine, links to every special interest you could imagine (Adult travel, Animal Watch, Cooking Schools, Learning Vacations, you name it).
- **www.pathfinder.com/travel/TL/tarticles/1132.html**
  Fifty tips for women traveling alone. They are quite simple but also very sound.
- **www.womenstravelclub.com/tips.html#street**
  Excellent safety and packing tips.

Nude Resorts and Beaches

Let's face it. You're 40 years old and probably have never been to a nude beach. Don't you think it's about time? Here is a list of some and I bet you can find one not too far from where you live (or perhaps you'd prefer one really far from where you live).

www.tanr.com
The Trade Association for Nude Recreation with quite extensive lists of resorts plus newsletters and the usual rationalizations of why being naked is so great. You know, the completely free feeling, the natural healthy experience, the fresh air, getting to see lots of naked people.

www.bareaffair.com
This company books travel arrangements to nude and clothing optional resorts around the world.

www.bluebonnetnudistpark.com/baredare
The Bare As You Dare 5K cross-country race. Get fit and run around naked at the same time.

www.sfbg.com/Nude/index.html
A directory of California nude beaches. Find the ones where all the stars hang out.

www.nudebeachguide.com
Nude beaches of the Northeast. Can you believe, even in New England?

sffb.com
South Florida nude beaches. I thought they were all nude in south Miami.

www.aanr.com
The American Association For Nude Recreation is surely looking for 40 year old people to join and expand the intellectual horizons of the organization. Along with other advice they explain that it's proper nude etiquette to always carry your own towel to sit upon.

Gambling Junkets

- **www.casinotours.com**
  This travel company organizes gambling junkets to casinos all around the U.S. and Caribbean.
- **www.casinojunkets.com**
  Casino junkets to Costa Rica.
- **www.4casino.com/links.htm**
  If you want to gamble this site has a handicapping service, junkets, computer gambling directory and more.
- **www.pokerandcasino.com/poker.htm**
  Serious poker playing in Costa Rica and casino gambling as well.
- **www.americasline.com**
  The odds and point spreads and all the information you need to make the right choices.
- **www.gambling-systems.com/books.html**
  Gambling books online. If you are going to be losing money you might as well know the odds.
- **www.smartgaming.com/index.htm**
  The Gambling Digest with articles and tips and systems.

As long as you don't have a gambling problem as discussed on page 27 you're allowed to go into these sites and plan a gambling junket. If you become a big player, I hear the casinos pick up the tabs for all your travel. Good luck.

Sports

At 40 it's time to learn some new sports. The touch football and pick up basketball games are going to kill you and leave you swallowing Advil and soaking in hot tubs. First I've listed the participant sports and then, if you feel old enough to become a complete couch potato, the spectator sports.

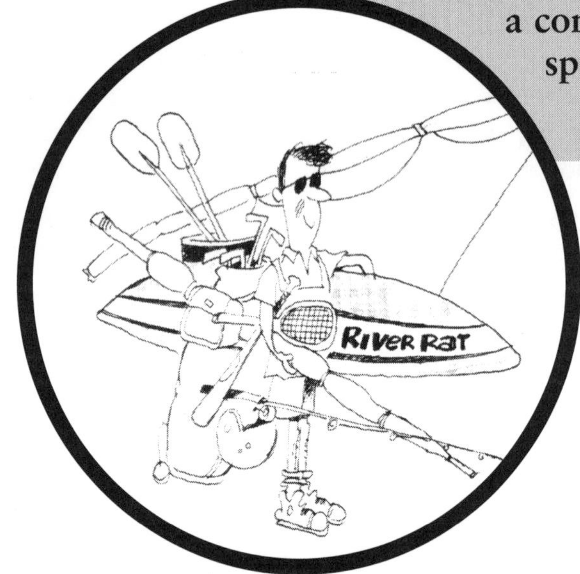

Golf

- **www.golfweb.com**
  Golf lessons online along with lots of tournament information, gear ratings, and a pro shop.
- **www.golfcourse.com**
  Reviews on over 16,000 courses. "So much golf so little time."
- **golfcircuit.com/cgi-bin/datasearch/bottom.html**
  Stats from the circuit, instruction, a golf search engine, plus the inevitable pro shop.
- **www.msnbc.com/news/golf1_front.asp**
  NBC Sport's golf coverage with all the latest results.
- **www.pgaonline.com**
  The official PGA site with audio coverage of the championships.
- **golf.traveller.com/golf**
  Traveler's golf information center with 2,000 courses, scorecard archives, and golf associations.

Of all the activities suited to 40 year olds, golf is one of the best. While the psychological frustration level can be extreme, the physical stress level is safe, the camaraderie superb and you can win lots of money playing with people seeking your favor. These sites will keep you up-to-date with the sport as well as providing information on courses all over the world.

Golf Equipment

Buying the equipment is as much fun as playing to many people and finding the latest club that is going to enhance your game or the ball guaranteed not to hook probably occupies more of these people's time than lessons. If you're one of them, and I count myself among you, these sites will be a joy.

- **www.golfandtennisworld.com**
  Golf and Tennis equipment. They promise lowest prices and over 20,000 items in stock. No way you could lose that many balls.
- **www.mvp.com**
  High quality golf and other sports equipment along with expert advice on what to buy.
- **www.clubstest.com**
  They claim unbiased ratings of all golf clubs plus up to the minute tournament stats and leaderboards.
- **www.mygolf.com**
  They sure have a load of golf products and claim the lowest prices on the web.
- **www.golfcoop.com**
  This is a non profit coop of golfers who have banded together to get the best prices for their group. You have to register before getting the prices.

Golf Magazines

- **www.golfdigest.com**
  Golf Digest's online site with more golf information than you can use.
- **www.golftoday.co.uk**
  Europe's premier online golf magazine.
- **www.golfmagazine.com**
  Golf Magazine's online site. If you have a day too rainy to play you can easily spend it surfing this site.
- **www.golfandtravel.com**
  There are some incredibly beautiful golf course photos on this site and you are going to want to visit them.
- **www.golfillustrated.com**
  There seem to be more golf magazines than telephone solicitors at dinner time. The sites don't carry the entire publication but you can probably glean all the information you'll ever need by just scanning several of them. It makes me wonder who bothers to subscribe when so much is available for free.
- **www.golftips.com**
  Some pretty good tips on improving your game.
- **www.travelandleisuregolf.com**
  Who has time to play golf when all these magazines are vying for your attention.

There are many golf magazines and, in addition to news about the sport, they are a wonderful source for tips on improving your game. I, for one, could never get anything out of pictures of swings and hip rotations and weight shifts but perhaps you can understand this stuff.

Fishing

There is a peace and beauty in fishing that combines with the excitement of the chase which makes it one of the favorite pastimes of 40 year olds. When you are over 40 your brains should have developed enough to at least match those of a stupid fish. An additional benefit is that fishing activities rarely require chiropractic care.

- **www.fishandgame.com**
  A comprehensive site that delivers fish reports, articles, travel and marketplace information.
- **www.flyfishingjournal.com**
  Tips, product reviews, fly tying, stream reports and lots more.
- **www.flyshop.com**
  Online fishing magazine with good articles, fish reports, classifieds, tide tables, etc.
- **www.acc.umu.se/~widmark/lwmanufa.html**
  A list of a zillion fishing equipment manufacturers. Just click on any one and you'll usually find their whole line. An incredible site.
- **fishingequipment.com**
  This site has links to absolutely every kind of fishing equipment and every kind of fishing site imaginable. Go here - you don't need me.

Fly Fishing

- **flyfishing.com**
  This very comprehensive resource has information on tying, shops, books, classifieds, lodges and more.
- **flyfishing.about.com/sports/flyfishing**
  Everything you need to know to find and catch them.
- **www.azlink.com/~jshannon/flygloss.html**
  Fly fishing glossary of terms. Now you have to learn all these words.
- **www.myhost.com/flyfishing101**
  A beginner's guide to fly fishing equipment, techniques, tying and more.
- **www.flyfishamerica.com**
  Online edition of Fly Fish America Magazine with lots of excellent articles.
- **www.flyshop.com**
  This online magazine has loads of stories and directories.

This is the "in" sport of the 90's. Everyone is fly fishing and here you have a sport that combines the outdoor excitement of the chase with the finesse and skill of an artist. Besides that you can tie your own flies on rainy afternoons and feel real "arts and crafty."

Boating

Get yourself a captain's cap because when you are 40 and the wind's in your face you'll make a striking captain. The boat's needs may dominate your free time and suck up money like the hole in the water it is, but until you buy a boat you'll have no idea how many friends you have. This applies whether your activity is fishing, skiing, or just driving around.

- **www.boating.com**
  Tides and tips, weather, buoys and boat shows. An all purpose boating site.
- **www.usps.org/usps.html**
  The United States Power Squadron.
- **www.powerboatmag.com**
  Online edition of Powerboat Magazine with ratings, boating news and classifieds.
- **www.boatshow.com**
  This is like a super boat show online. The equivalent of 2,000 pages of details on boats and equipment.
- **www.boater.com**
  Charter, repairs, tips, books, and classifieds.
- **www.allaboutboats.com**
  Boats for sale, boating events, fishing and lots of links to more boating information.
- **www.motorboatingandsailing.com**
  Excerpts from Motor Boating and Sail Magazine with tips, equipment reviews and links.
- **www.boatfacts.com/home.asp**
  Articles are available from a dozen boating magazines plus classifieds, specs and other information.

Sailing

- **sailing.about.com/sports/sailing/index.htm**
  Links to everything about sailing from about.com.
- **www.sailnet.com**
  Hundreds of articles and resources for the sailor.
- **www.yachtworld.com**
  A boating yellow pages with 17,000 marine businesses. Truly everything is here. Thousands of boats for sale.
- **www.sailnet.com/sailing**
  Sailing Magazine's home site with some articles available from each issue.
- **www.sailingworld.com/swdeckpg.htm**
  Cruising and Sailing World online magazine with race reports, calendar and racing information.
- **www.american-sailing.com**
  American Sailing Assoc. with books and schools and standards for the sport.
- **sailing.info-access.com**
  Marine weather and tide information, sailor's bulletin board, discussion groups and race calendars.

Sailing itself isn't really difficult. It's learning all the nautical terms that's a bitch. While you may think the wind's power is free, you'll realize differently when you buy a sailboat and start replacing sails and lost winch handles.

Biking

It's your choice. You can be efficient with an aerodynamic position, hard seat, stiff bike and sore body or comfy with an upright position and plush equipment. Unless you have retained all your competitive instincts the comfy option is going to feel much better.

- **www.biking.com**
  Ten thousand bike products for sale plus biking articles and people.
- **www.dfwnetmall.com/cybersports/bicycle.htm**
  An introduction to biking for novices including buying a bike, maintenance and other information.
- **www.bicyclingmagazine.com**
  Online version of the leading biking magazine.
- **www.cycling.org**
  This is quite a site and can link you to any manufacturer as well as directions to any bike shop.
- **www.backroads.com**
  Backroads offers the largest and among the best bike tours worldwide.
- **www.gorp.com/gorp/activity/biking/bik_guid.htm**
  An excellent guide to bike trails and tours throughout the U.S.
- **www.sevencycles.com**
  They are expensive, but these guys make the best custom bikes in the world. I own one.

Aerobic Exercise

- **www.cybercise.com/dyna.html**
  All kinds of music for aerobic exercising in case you don't already have enough tapes and disks.
- **www.fitness-factory.com/english/index.html**
  You can download choreography videos and they must give the cost somewhere but it was hidden too cleverly for me to find.
- **www.bodytrends.com/gourley.htm**
  Basic aerobic exercise principles. This is good information.
- **www.iwr.com/chimachine/**
  This is another lulu. You buy this "Chi Machine" for only $480 and you plug it in and lie down and 5 minutes is equal to a mile walk. If you accidentally fall asleep you could end up, skinny as could be, in China.
- **k2.kirtland.cc.mi.us/~balbachl/cardio.htm**
  A simple and factual explanation about using aerobic exercises to lose weight.
- **mrmac-jr.scs.unr.edu/jenscott/Fitness.html**
  It'll take you a minute to read the ten reasons why aerobic exercise is important and they're all true.

You can get in your workout in any weather and you should get plenty of inspiration from your tape or instructor. If you are good or brave you can wear your tight lycra up front and if a bit out of shape can hide in baggy sweats at the back of the class.

Running

It wouldn't seem you'd need lots of equipment and instruction to just run but that's the kind of world we live in now. Special shoes, special shorts, magazines, coaches and heart monitors just to mention a few. Selecting a running shoe to match your style can take an entire weekend.

www.running.com
This site leads you to just about everything you could ever need to know about running.

www.americanrunning.org
The American Running Assoc. hosts a terrific site that lets you easily find information on all aspects of running, equipment and training.

www.runningnetwork.com
An excellent review of running shoes.

www.runningtips.com
Some good basic running tips.

runningshoes.com/hp.php3
Prices on some major brands of running shoes.

www.cybernude.com/nuderuns
Calendar of nude running events. I thought I'd throw this in just to keep you inspired.

Weight Lifting

- **members.xoom.com/duranman**
  A good introduction to strength training and bodybuilding.
- **ftp.cray.com/pub/misc.fitness/misc.fitness.faq.html**
  A fabulous site that answers questions and gives advice on every conceivable kind of exercise. If you have to look at one site on fitness make it this one.
- **www.worldguide.com/Fitness/stex.html**
  More strength training exercises, with instructions and photos, than you could do in a month of Sundays.
- **www.lastingresults.com**
  This site offers very concise and sound advice and a very practical list of 10 weight exercises.
- **www.thriveonline.com/shape/weights/weights.intro.html**
  Eight essential good basic weight exercises for beginners.
- **www.naturalstrength.com**
  The source for strength training information with no hype and no bull.

After 40 the tone in your upper body starts to deteriorate. Well actually it started to deteriorate after you stopped playing sports in high school but it becomes much more noticeable after 40. The most efficient way to exercise the hundreds of muscles in your body, short of doing manual labor as your main job, is by lifting weights. Learn something about it here.

Scuba Diving

Scuba diving and snorkeling are great sports for 40 year olds. They are relatively stress free on your muscle and bone structure, and health wise all you have to worry about is being eaten by sharks, having your ear drums blown out by pressure and drowning a black horrible death. Fortunately these things don't happen too often and thankfully, not so far, on any of my dives.

www.scubacentral.com
A good general site that has a tremendous amount of information including equipment reviews, learning to dive, places to dive, chat, and great photographs.

www.mtsinai.org/pulmonary/books/scuba/contents.htm
This is a very comprehensive book that explains all aspects of scuba diving.

www.scubadiving.com/gear
Rodale's Scuba Diving Magazine site with excellent reviews of equipment and dive spots along with articles on photography and all aspects of the sport.

www.padi.com
Padi, one of the main certification services, maintains this site with information on all of their courses and details on diving travel.

www.3routes.com/scuba/index.html
This site tries to list every dive resort and live aboard in the world. They list over 4,000 and have reviews of many.

Miscellaneous Sports

www.campnetamerica.com
A great source of everything you need to know about camping and campsites in case you absolutely insist on sleeping in the woods rather than a motel.

www.hunting.com
Information on hunting licenses and equipment, apparel, footwear etc. Be careful not to shoot the campers.

www.geocities.com/Colosseum/Sideline/5762
This extensive directory lists more martial arts than you ever dreamed existed and it takes a brave 40 year old to start karate at this age.

www.bowl.com
Championships, news, links, coaching and everything else you can think of about bowling.

www.swiminfo.com
The latest race results, workouts and techniques, a good buyer's guide, swim camps, all time records, and probably cures for athlete's foot.

skicentral.com
A ski site that seems to have everything including almost 6,000 snowsport sites, equipment, racing, daily ski guides and even a web cam at the top of Mt. Washington.

We must have lots of leisure time in the modern world because there are an incredible profusion of sports to both do and watch not to mention hobbies and vacations. The internet alone could probably suck up most of the rest of your life and you couldn't even get through the "A's".

Football

Here is a sport that has taken over most fans' Sunday and Monday nights not to even mention college games on Saturday. Where else can a guy enjoy a beer, relive his high school football days, watch a game and make money as well if he gets the point spread right.

- **www.msnbc.com/news/NFL_Front.asp**
  The latest NFL news from MSNBC.
- **www.dickbutkus.com/dbfn**
  Dick Butkis Football Network covering everything from NFL to Pop Warner.
- **www.nflplayers.com**
  NFL players home pages, analysis and news.
- **www.sportserver.com/SportServer/football**
  Football news, college and professional.
- **www.ultimatefootballshop.com**
  The ultimate football shop where you can buy authentic football apparel from Sports Illustrated and the NFL.
- **www.cnnsi.com/football/college/conferences/acc**
  Sports Illustrated and CNN combine to offer team profiles, scores, news, statistics standings and schedules.

Baseball

- **www.msnbc.com/news/MLB_Front.asp**
  The latest baseball news from MSNBC.
- **www.baseball.com**
  Scores, news, team web sites, everything.
- **www.heavyhitter.com/default.asp**
  This baseball search engine will help you find anything about the game.
- **www.totalbaseball.com**
  The official baseball encyclopedia with statistics, player profiles, history, chat, store and whatever.
- **www.majorleaguebaseball.com**
  The official site of Major League Baseball. Schedules, scores, stats, team profiles and all the rest.
- **www.sportingnews.com/baseball/sluggers**
  A list of baseball's 50 greatest sluggers from Sporting News.

You may have to drive your kids to soccer games but baseball is still the all-American pastime and it's something to enjoy on TV or at a ballpark.

Basketball

You don't necessarily bet, and they don't often get bloody, so basketball must be the intellectual major sport that appeals to the more sophisticated 40 year olds among us as well as those over 6' tall who did well in the game when 6' meant something.

- **www.basketball.com**
  Everything about basketball from the NBA to the cheerleader of the day.
- **www.msnbc.com/msn/NBA2.asp?cp1=1**
  Current news about the NBA from MSNBC.
- **www.usabasketball.com**
  The men's and women's national teams as well as Olympic information.
- **www.finalfour.net**
  The official site of the NCAA basketball championships.
- **cnnsi.com/basketball/college/**
  CNN and Sports Illustrated coverage of men's and women's college basketball.
- **hwww.hoophall.com**
  Basketball's Hall of Fame with all the exhibits, stories and history.
- **www.bbhighway.com**
  A site for coaches to improve their skill along with all the usual information about games and players.

Hockey

- **www.hockey.com**
  Hockey news, stats, scores and everything.
- **proicehockey.about.com/sports/proicehockey**
  Scores, news, player profiles, and fights.
- **www.thn.com**
  Online edition of The Hockey News.
- **www.nhl.com**
  The official NHL site with stats, news, scores and history.
- **www.hockeydb.com**
  An archive of hockey information dating back to the 1920's.
- **www.inthecrease.com**
  Comprehensive coverage of major, minor and international hockey.

The speed of the game alone has a tremendous appeal and the action and amazing hand-eye coordination has many claiming that this is the most athletic of the major sports. The fights, while less than in the old days, are still great to watch especially if you don't get boxing on your cable.

Car Racing

Car Racing has come to mean going to a track and taking lessons, not speeding to the beach while watching for your radar detector to go off. These schools are authentic but expensive. More sensible, of course, is to let someone else risk their car and body and you just watch the race on TV.

- **www.nascar.com**
  The official Nascar site with schedules, standings and news.
- **espn.go.com/auto**
  Covers Formula One, Nascar, Indy, CART, NHRA with schedules, standings and results.
- **www.na-motorsports.com**
  North American Motorsports. All kinds of racing and rally and hill climbs, race driving schools, news and discussions.
- **www.scca.org/index.html**
  The Sport Car Club of America lets you in on club racing and rallies. You don't get speeding tickets here, you get trophies.
- **www.racesearch.com**
  When you want to speed up your old sedan to pull away from the state troopers, this is the site that can outfit you.
- **www.usatoday.com/sports/motor/autos.htm**
  USA Today coverage of all phases of racing and schedules.

Boxing

- **www2.xtdl.com/~brasslet**
  Internet boxing records archive. Biographies and records of all active boxers and all time greats. Truly everything about the fighters.
- **www.sportingnews.com/boxing**
  Boxing news and previews from this online magazine.
- **www.cyberboxingzone.com**
  This is a fun site for online boxing news with all sorts of historical information as well as streaming video and sound clips. A good rainy afternoon's entertainment.
- **www.ipcress.com/writer/boxing.html**
  Boxing on the web brings you rules, rankings, news and statistics.
- **www.boxingranks.com**
  Honest Howie's boxing ratings, predictions and latest boxing news.

A great spectator sport, enjoyed mostly by guys, that has become even more available with cable TV. Invite friends over and smoke cigars, drink and gamble. It'll make you feel good.

Homes, Cars and Clothing

Every 40 year old is a purchasing agent making daily decisions on what to buy and how much to spend. I can't begin to cover all your buying decision needs, but have listed a few fun things and a few major ones in this section. Some general advice? When buying a car never be hesitant to walk out; and when buying intimate apparel do it in a neighborhood where they won't recognize you.

Real Estate

- **www.domania.com**
  If you're buying, selling or just looking, this site provides all the tools and information of prices, values, taxes etc. It has an enormous archive of home sales.

- **realestate.yahoo.com**
  You can search the real estate market nationwide for a home based on your criteria and compare cities based on things like cost, crime and income.

- **www.realtor.com**
  With over 1 million listings this site lets you find a neighborhood, realtor and lender. They will even estimate your monthly mortgage payments.

- **www.ziprealty.com**
  They claim to be the first online real estate brokers and will give you access to loans, home inspection, insurance and, oh yes, homes.

- **www.owners.com**
  You can list your own home for $99 to $289 and avoid paying 6% to a broker.

- **www.forsalebyowner.com**
  Another sale-by-owner service which offers various deals for listing your house.

You can snoop and see what your new neighbors paid for the place down the street and really speed up your own real estate buying or selling with the internet. Don't forget to have the freshly baked bread smell in your house when you're selling.

Men's Clothing and Fashion

Who has time to go shopping? You may have to try on suits (if you still wear them) or shoes, but accessories are easy to buy online. Send the stuff back if your kids don't think they're cool.

www.dailynewsrecord.com
The Daily News Record is the men's fashion magazine and while it is meant for the trade if you are serious about keeping up with trends this will help you. Otherwise you'll be bored to death.

www.firstview.com/mendesignerlist/Gucci.html
Runway fashions from Gucci, no less. Most 40 year olds would have to be pretty brave to wear this stuff.

www.costumegallery.com/men.htm
The history of men's wear this century. See if any of the outfits you're still wearing are historical (or hysterical).

www.landsend.com
A super mail order company that has a fine range of casual clothes, dress shirts and accessories.

www.brooksbrothers.com
Check out Brooks Brothers and at least you'll know what you should be wearing.

Women's Clothing

www.tallclassics.com
If you are over 5' 10", this is the place for you.

www.wwd.com
Women's Wear Daily. The horse's mouth.

www.worldmedia.fr/fashion
Haute couture designers and their collections.

www.fashion.net
Fashion news, chat, runway videos and shopping.

www.silhouettes.com
A large selection for full figured women.

Shopping is so much fun, most women can always find the time. The internet is a good way to keep up with styles and order the kind of accessories or specialty items that most stores can't stock. It's also great for buying sexy items for which

you're too embarrassed to go into local stores.

www.godess.com
Detailed global fashion news. You can also click around and get world news from anywhere.

www.catalogsite.com
A cataloging of catalogs. Over 200 catalogs shown by the top 10 or by interest.

www.apparel.net/index.cgi
What's new, what's cool, designers, catalogs, manufacturers and lots of clothing.

www.7thonsixth.com
One of those pain in the behind sites that you can't get rid of. I think it has information on all the fashion shows. Don't bother unless you're ready to unplug your computer.

www.theoutdoorwoman.com
Women's sporting apparel and accessories. Even if you don't hunt or fish you can look cool and impress your friends.

fashion.about.com/style/fashion/msub13.htm
There is so much on this site I always find it a little overwhelming but the advice and tips and fashion trends are sound.

www.styleclick.com
Search through hundreds of brands in this online catalog each showing their line. It would seem this site could clothe the world.

Household Furniture

You can't sit on the chairs or slide the drawers in and out but once you know what you want the selection and discounted prices on the net can't be beat.

- **www.crateandbarrel.com**
  Furniture and accessories for your home from Crate and Barrel.
- **www.homefurnish.com/buy_menu.htm**
  A guide to understanding the quality of wood and upholstered furniture as well as what different pieces are best for.
- **www.cherryhillfurn.com/c3.html**
  Some more good advice on understanding furniture and what to look for in determining quality.
- **www.furnishingsfinder.com**
  This is a useful site. Pick the room, furniture and price you're looking for and up pops a list of manufacturer's sites to visit.
- **www.geocities.com/Heartland/7400/furniture.html**
  How to buy furniture at discount prices from all the main manufacturers in North Carolina.
- **www.ianr.unl.edu/pubs/homefurnish/g1247.htm**
  Excellent discussion of what to look for and how wood furniture is made.
- **www.furniture.com**
  You can view much more furniture on a site like this than any store can carry. It's an excellent way to plan.

Decorating

When it's time to give the ratty old couch to the Salvation Army and change the color of the drapes, check out these sites and become an accomplished decorator. You can do it. Everyone's taste is so different that you can get away with anything if you have the guts.

hg.women.com/homeandgarden/decor/index.htm?msns
Decorating 101. An expert's guide to adorning your abode plus endless decorating information.

interiordec.about.com/homegarden/interiordec
About.com has sites offering so many other things that I have stayed away from them. This one certainly has a wonderful list of decorating subjects.

www5.electriciti.com/todesign/report12.htm
This site sells decorating books and they have a free report on defining your style which is an excellent place to start your planning.

www.designaroom.com
What a fun site. You can create a room and fill it with furniture and move everything around to try it all out. Fabulous.

www.dir-dd.com/mainpage.html
Thousands of showpiece images from interior decorators, home furnishing resources, and antique dealers.

www.thehome.com
You will get a wonderful education on this site about furniture, floors and other subjects.

www.furniturefind.com
This is quite an extensive furniture site with excellent pictures of major lines for every room in your house plus electronics and claims of large discounts.

www.decoratingstudio.com
A vast site with lots of advice but also staggeringly complete links to suppliers for everything imaginable in your home.

Tools

Most guys love buying tools and hanging out in hardware stores. We may never use the stuff we buy but it's nice to have them "just in case". Here are a bunch of tool catalogs that you can peruse on your computer. It's fun to have a package or two arrive every now and then with more tools, and then you can buy more gadgets to hang them up with.

- **www.garrettwade.com**
  Really beautiful woodworking tools.
- **www.toolsforless.com**
  They claim bargain prices on brand name power tools.
- **www.woodcraft.com/woodcraft/homepage.asp**
  An online catalog of woodworking tools.
- **www.toolbazaar.co.uk/tools_sale.htm**
  A really neat site in England selling antique tools.
- **www.housemart.com/refer1.asp**
  With 35,000 tools you can spend all Sunday afternoon here.
- **www.northwestpowertools.com**
  You'll find everything here from generators to jointers.
- **www.northerntool.com**
  This catalog has hand and power tools but also a superb collection of generators, motors, garden equipment, and home construction stuff.

Car Buying Information

- **www.autosite.com**
  A great site with dealer invoice prices, used car values, photos, specs and everything else to help you buy a car.
- **www.aautomall.com**
  Automall searches over 600 dealers and lets you email them for quotes on the car you want. It also has information on warranties, insurance and everything else involved with buying a car.
- **www.carprice.com**
  Car, truck and motorcycle pricing guide and information on negotiating, recalls, insurance, leasing, rebates and all.
- **www.caranddriver.com**
  Car and Driver magazine's online site with excellent car reviews and articles. Check out their 10 best cars of the year.

If sales people treated you like an idiot or refused to bargain the last time you bought a car, you are in for a pleasant surprise. You can go in now armed with all their costs and knowledge about the options. They'll probably still treat you like an idiot but now you can walk out and buy the car on the internet and possibly even see it in your driveway tomorrow.

- **www.autobytel.com**
  Invoice prices, safety records and car reviews make it easy for you to buy a car.
- **www.dealernet.com**
  There are almost 7,000 dealers represented here. Check out free quotes from one near your home.
- **www.nhtsa.dot.gov**
  Your government provides lots of information on the safety of vehicles and other life saving concerns. It is worth checking out before selecting as car.
- **www.kbb.com**
  The famous Kelly Blue Book gives you the used car values that the dealers laugh at and you can never get when you try to sell it yourself.
- **www.carorder.com**
  You can pick the options you want and actually buy the car at this site.

Car Repairing

You can't have the old buggy repaired on the net but you can get enough free advice to do it yourself or at least talk intelligently with the Service Manager for all the good that'll do you.

- **www.cskauto.com**
  Maintenance tips plus a place to buy all the parts you break trying to fix the parts that are broken.
- **library.thinkquest.org/19199**
  Great online courses on how your car works. These courses range from those for novices to professional repairmen.
- **www.autosite.com/garage/garmenu.asp**
  With this repair encyclopedia and troubleshooting guide even your wife will be able to fix cars.
- **www.allexperts.com/browse.asp?Meta=12**
  An incredibly valuable site where you can submit questions on car repair and get an email response from experts.
- **www.haynes.com**
  This is the place to buy your Haynes Manual with detailed repair information on almost any car.
- **www.autorepairconsultant.net**
  A free general question consulting service that will answer your questions by email. They charge $25 for specific printed material and training.

Intimate Apparel

- **www.victoriassecret.com**
  The women in Victoria's Secret catalog are truly world class.
- **www.imt.net/~lingerie/index.html**
  Custom tailored intimates.
- **www.lingerie-store.com**
  The descriptions are in French as well as English so it must be sexy.
- **www.lingeriemart.com**
  They claim to be the largest source for all kinds of wholesale lingerie and from the size of their site I can believe it.
- **www.shoptheplaza.com/playstor/4ever.html**
  A large selection of sexy and erotic lingerie.
- **www.lusciouswear.com**
  Very sexy fine lingerie.
- **emporium.net/avalon**
  "Drift to a place where romance and innocence meet."
- **www.business.mcmaster.ca/courses/s727/ davio/bridal.htm**
  Bridal peignoir sets, lace chiffon charmeuse gowns, baby doll sets and such.

Guys love these sites and women who are busy or shy can shop here for some of the sexiest outfits imaginable. They are guaranteed to make your sex life more exciting.

Bathroom Remodeling

If you are like me, you spend happy hours in your bathroom either contemplating weighty matters, reading, wallowing in a tub or even doing your necessary business. There is no sense spending all this time in uncomfortable surroundings and these sites will show you just what kind of luxury is possible. It's a good place to spend money since all real estate brokers say it increases the value of your home.

www.kitchen-bath.com/bbasics.htm
Bathroom design basics in case you are interested in a remodeling job. Check out the "toiletarium" section if you feel like I do about this part of the bathroom.

www.us.amstd.com/scripts
If you want to view some luxury bathrooms the American Standard site is a nice place to start your dreaming.

www.hometime.com/projects/ktchbath.htm
All the how-to information if you are planning a remolding bathroom job. Don't forget the saunas, spas and steam rooms.

www.nkba.org
The National Kitchen and Bath Assoc. gives you worthwhile tips on remodeling as well as links to manufacturers.

www.bathweb.com
A complete directory to the bathroom industry. You can find everything here including group bathtubs.

Financial and Legal Sites

You're 40. It's time to think about finances and retirement and to start managing your resources more seriously. You just can't go through life spending all your money on clothes and computer gadgets. These sites will teach you about investing, a little law, insurance and perhaps a new career of money management. Don't go crazy and quit your job before reading everything.

Employment

Time for a midlife crisis? Ready to tell off your boss and move to a fast track in a new company? Now is the time. There's an unprecedented amount of employment information on the internet and if you don't get the raise you think you deserve or if your stock options go under water you can probably quickly find a new job.

content.careers.msn.com/gh.cfm
Good hints on resumés, interviews and negotiating offers. You'll feel so confident reading this you just might quit.

midcareer.monster.com
A monster employment site that lists hundreds of thousands of jobs. Somebody out there must be looking for you.

www.careermosaic.com
You can post a resumé here or search under whatever criteria you wish.

www.careerweb.com
Good career guidance that I hope you don't need, plus the usual resumé and job searches.

www.looksmart.com/r?page=/dls/ca/ca.html
LookSmart's career center with 150,000 listings and lots of ways to search and post your resumé.

www.flipdog.com/home.html
The internet's largest data base of job openings with each listing direct from an employer.

Stocks and Investments

- **moneycentral.msn.com/investor/research/welcome.asp**
  Money Central's stock research tool with lots of information on just about every company that's traded.
- **www.nyse.com**
  New York Stock Exchange quotes, listings and links to the listed companies.
- **www.nasdaq.com**
  All the information for stocks, indexes and companies listed on the NASDAQ.
- **dowjones.wsj.com/p/main.html**
  The Dow Jones index, its products and services.
- **www.cnbc.com**
  Business information, stock reports, a ticker search engine and financial data.
- **www.cnnfn.com**
  CNN financial news.

At 40 you wholeheartedly subscribe to the concept that stocks are your best investment for the long term. It's been true in the past, but the stock market does have a way of always surprising people. With these sites you can at least keep an eye on what's happening and sound intelligent at cocktail parties.

Stocks and Investments

With the vast amount of financial information on the internet, every 40 year old dodo can have the tools to make intelligent investment decisions provided you make the effort to study and understand. Remember, you are competing against professionals who spend all day analyzing this information, not just a few hours on the weekend, and who have a network of buddies providing inside intelligence.

- **www.etrade.com**
  Get in on the next Microsoft, Intel or Cisco and leave millions to your college for a new athletic center.
- **www.smartmoney.com**
  All the same market information all over again. There must be money here someplace because there sure are a lot of sites.
- **www.mfea.com**
  The mutual fund investor's center with lots of information on mutual funds and 100 definitions that you'd better learn before you start to seek your fortune.
- **www.hoovers.com/ipo/0,1334,23,00.html**
  IPO Central. Get in on a "sure thing" with Initial Public Offerings.
- **www.bigcharts.com**
  Charts of all the companies plus interactive charts to help you make your investment decisions.

Financial

- **www.cfol.com**
  This is the world's largest business and financial search engine.
- **www.financialweb.com**
  If you can absorb as much financial information as this site offers, you must be in the investment business already.
- **www.expertstocktrader.com**
  They promise fast execution of your trades at low prices.
- **www.bay-street.com**
  Financial resources for the individual investor.
- **www.fool.com/radio/radio.htm**
  The Motley Fool takes an unconventional approach to investing and going against the conventional thinking is often the smartest way to invest. I like this site.

The overwhelming amount of data on the internet is enough to make me happy to turn the whole thing over to my broker. If you do invest on your own, one good bet would be to specialize in a few small companies where it is possible for you to become the expert. Good luck and please don't call me with sure fire tips.

Mutual Funds

These sites will give you a good overlook of mutual funds, their performance, who is running them, their focus and fees. Go ahead if you want, leave your investment decisions to a 27 year old kid who has never seen a down market and probably just bought a new BMW with your commissions.

www.standardandpoors.com/onfunds
Standard & Poor's Select Funds is an exclusive designation that indicates a fund has passed rigorous standards for continuity of performance and management.

www.fundalarm.com
This free site rings the alarm when managers change or funds change ownership. It's good stuff to know.

www.fundsinteractive.com
The web's top rated fund site with everything from fund basics to news to profiles of managers. Links to 120 mutual fund groups.

www.fundz.com
The top 10 load and non-load funds, all the major ratings of funds performance, research, top 40 fund internet sites and such.

members.aol.com/plweiss1/mfunds.htm
Mutual Funds Made Simple. Practical guidance on investing money, terminology, questions and answers and other information for beginning and intermediate investors.

Entrepreneurship

- **www.liraz.com**
  You can take a test and see if you have what it takes to be an entrepreneur, though it's pretty simplistic. They also sell entrepreneurial books and CD Roms.

- **entrepreneurs.about.com/smallbusiness/entrepreneurs**
  Lots of basics and good tips. Start reading this stuff before quitting your job.

- **www.entrepreneurmag.com**
  This online magazine has so many articles on starting and running your own business that you'll have to quit your regular job just to read them all.

- **www.score.org**
  This organization works in conjunction with the Small Business Administration and provides free advice to small companies from retired executives.

- **www.sba.gov/sbdc**
  Your government's Small Business Administration will give you money and advice and tips and brochures and counseling. Well, maybe they won't give you money.

- **www.businessnet.freeservers.com**
  "Free" advice for starting an online business so you too can go public and be a billionaire.

If you are going to do it, now is the time. Open that inn in Vermont or start the dot com in your garage. Live your dream before it becomes too late.

Law

If you have ever been involved in a legal dispute you know how expensive lawyers can be. It is very often even more expensive to think you are a lawyer and try to do it yourself. Actually you can't win and that is why everyone feels the way they do about lawyers and there are so many "lawyer" jokes. Practicing law by yourself can be dangerous, but running to your lawyer for every decision will bankrupt you. The best approach is to have one of your kids go to law school and advise you for free.

www.lawyers.com/lawyers-com/content/hiring.html
Good tips on hiring a lawyer and even advice on what it will cost.

www.abanet.org/referral/home.html
If you need a lawyer the American Bar Assoc. will give you the names of a few million.

freeadvice.com
This site offers answers to about 3,000 legal questions, but if you have a good personal injury case they'll probably be at your door before you can turn your computer off.

www.lawyers.com/lawyers-com/executable/ask
Some very good answers to legal questions. At least one good lawyer dedicated his or her time to this site.

www.law.cornell.edu
If you are really ready to be your own lawyer, this site gives you good pointers with constitutions, codes, court opinions and even ethics.

www.legaldocs.com
Write your own wills and leases. Save money and only get into trouble later (just kidding). Some forms are free and others from $3.50 to $27.75.

Women in Business

- **www.onlinewbc.org**
  Learn about entrepreneurship and business, running your own business, exchanging information and online business help from the Small Business Association.
- **www.bizresource.com**
  Support and information for small business owners and aspiring entrepreneurs. Newsletters, advice and tips.
- **www.e-magnify.com**
  Integrates education, business and career resources for women. Good basic advice on starting, expanding and leveraging your business.
- **www.bizplan.com**
  Help on creating a business plan with all the do's and don'ts.
- **www.womenconnect.com**
  Connecting women in business. A lot of good information on starting your own business.
- **www.bizwomen.com**
  Find business opportunities and develop networks and alliances with other women.

Guess what sisters? There is a whole network of us out there willing to help us start businesses and advance. Tune in and use every advantage you can get.

Taxes and More Financial Advice

If the IRS audits your return just tell them you got all your information off their site on the internet. They won't understand any better than you and they may let you off. Don't tell them I said so.

www.nysscpa.org/sound_advice/sound_advice.html
Weekly financial advice from CPA's.

www.financenter.com
All sorts of calculators for helping make decisions on buying a car, saving for college, budgeting, insurance and other things involving your money. A very useful site.

www.cnnfn.com
A very complete financial site that gives you all the tools you'll need for planning.

www.irs.gov
This site is run by the U.S. Treasury and they'd like to advise you to pay your taxes. I suppose they have interesting and useful information here but I just kept getting funny numbers.

www.irs.com
This commercial tax site is, at least user friendly. They provide useful links, forms and software; some are free some cost.

Insurance

- **www.insweb.com**
  This is a free service that lets you compare insurance quotes for leading companies to help you find the best rates.
- **www.farmersinsurance.com/fi3000.html**
  Farmers Insurance Company says they'll tell you all about insurance and I figured a farmer wouldn't lie so this is probably a good place to get information.
- **www.insure.com**
  More information about insurance than you are going to want. I think it's easier to just wait for the insurance salesman to call.
- **www.insuremarket.com**
  You can get quotes online which should be useful for comparing prices with what you're now paying.
- **www.insweb.com**
  Insurance is a confusing subject so I guess it pays to get some free education and quotes to compare from sites like this.

Insurance is something of a mystery business if there ever was one. These sites will let you get some competitive rates without having to listen to a pressure pitch from still another insurance agent.

Planning For Retirement

There's no need to live in a trailer and eat canned dog food after you retire if you just put a little away each week. These sites will show you just how little.

- **lifenet.com/ret_form.html**
  This retirement cash flow analyzer will show how long your bundle will last once you stop earning a paycheck. It gives you a starting point for realizing how much you're going to have to save.

- **www.usnews.com/usnews/issue/980629/29reti.htm**
  This site has some really solid retirement planning advice from U.S. News. You can believe them. They're not trying to sell you something.

- **retireplan.about.com/finance/retireplan**
  A very comprehensive site with lots of information on how to invest for retirement, planning guides, tax advantage retirement accounts and other "how-tos" of leaving the working rat race.

- **www.columbiafunds.com/interactive.html**
  The retirement estimating planner is fun. See how much you should be saving to keep from living in a shipping crate when you move to Florida.

- **www.quicken.com/retirement**
  This site from Quicken gives you all the tools you need to figure out just how much you're not going to be able to afford to save. 401 k's, Roth IRA, Keogh, pension plans, Social Security, they're all here.

- **www.sovereignbank.com/calculate/index.html**
  Over 75 calculators to help you figure everything from what it'll take to make you a millionaire to how long you should keep a car.

Food and Drink

By the time you're 40 you probably have established some strong preferences in what you eat and drink and have become a bit of an expert in your favorite wines or beer or Chinese food. Even so, you're going to love getting more information on delicious things to put in your stomach, and if these sites cause your eating and drinking to get a little out of hand you can always drop back to the Health and Fitness section and check on the latest diets.

Cooking

Expand your horizons beyond the fast food places your kids like with these sites and discover new taste temptations and new restaurants. Then gain weight, find out they all cause terrible diseases and start a new search. It's the cycle of modern man.

www.agrotrade.com
A fascinating place to shop for spices from around the world as well as tea, dried fruit and candies.

www.cornwellcoffee.com
Fresh Kona coffee direct from Hawaii. It sounds delicious.

www.cooking.com
The master site for cooking with lots of cooking gear for sale as well as recipes, products and techniques.

www.epicurious.com
Thousands of recipes, kitchen equipment, basic skills and even etiquette on eating an artichoke, among other things.

www.inquisitivecook.com
A super data base of answers to questions about cooking.

www.hoptechno.com/book1.htm
Dietary guidelines for Americans and splendid tips for healthy food preparation.

www.geocities.com/NapaValley/4079/index.html
The list of almost 20 online cooking magazines alone will keep you busy for the rest of your life. The history and legends of foods is fascinating and then there are the recipes.

Food Magazines

- **www.pathfinder.com/FoodWine**
  The online edition of Food and Wine with cooking, entertainment, Epicurean lifestyle, home decorating and wine reviews.

- **www.epicurious.com/b_ba/b00_home/ba.html**
  Bon Appetit's online version with recipes and techniques, beer and wine, restaurants and stuff. You can type in a search of whatever you find in your refrigerator and come up with great recipes.

- **www.gourmet.com**
  Tap into Gourmet Magazine's data base and you'll be eating imaginative new meals for the rest of your life.

- **www.cookinglight.com**
  Cooking Light Magazine will give you some healthy alternatives for all the weight you've been putting on with the other magazine recipes.

- **www.vrg.org/journal**
  Fabulous archives from the Vegetarian Journal with recipes that will keep you happily eating forever.

Tired of the same old dinners? There are probably more recipes on the internet than overweight people at a state fair. Enjoy and indulge by surfing through various ones and you'll soon discover sites with favorites that will enhance your eating pleasure and may even help your antacid problem.

Recipes

Here's your guide to thousands of new ideas and recipes of every type. You can't come up with creative and healthy meals if you're still using a 1980's cookbook. Perhaps you'll even get lucky and find something other than pizza and hamburgers that the kids will like.

www.epicurious.com
Features recipes from Bon Appetit and Gourmet Magazines. Data base of more than 10,000 recipes, searchable by keyword. Topical articles and guides to restaurants, cooking tools, seasonal cooking, and international eating.

www.allrecipes.com
Recipes by category, subdivided into additional categories (such as soups, vegetarian). Some recipes are rated. A recipe exchange too.

food.homearts.com/food
Part of Women.com's network, just choose from type of dish, ingredients, cuisine, how many calories, complexity of recipe and time to prepare, and the perfect recipes will be displayed. You can even get a recipe by just telling them what you have on hand in your refrigerator.

www.geocities.com/Tokyo/Market/7773
Asian Recipe, where you can browse through numerous Asian cuisines, from Malaysan hot curry to delicate sushi.

www.foodsales.com/recipe.html
Recipes in many categories.

Special Recipes

- **www.fatfree.com**
  3,766 low-fat, vegetarian recipes to choose from. Also features discussions, USDA nutrient database, a list of vegetarian restaurants world-wide, and much more.

- **www.vegweb.com**
  Vegetarian and vegan recipes, chat, veggie info, questions and answers, and a link to Amazon.com books. Even explains what TVP is.

- **hometown.aol.com/meadowscd/recipes/index.html**
  Debbie Meadow's favorite recipes.

- **www.recipecenter.com**
  More than 100,000 great vegetarian recipes. Recipe satisfaction guaranteed.

- **members.tripod.com/~peoplesreview/recipemovie.html**
  Each Thursday they post a new recipe and new movie suggestion.

- **www.planetveggie.com/bin/veggie.pl?item=1220-8**
  Vegetarian recipes for every course and every ingredient.

- **idt.net/~wordup/bread.html**
  This archive was started with the notion that although it is impossible to break bread with all the peoples of the world, at least we can share some recipes. Includes traditional recipes, bread machine recipes, and bread baking resources.

Vegetarians aren't the lunatic fringe your parents thought them. They're us. Everyone you know claims to "hardly ever" eat red meat. Whenever the "experts" study some grass eater in a third world country it seems they find some disease that we are all dying from and to which the locals are immune when they are not busy starving to death themselves.

Foreign Food Recipes

Every time there is a political upheaval someplace in the world the refugees rush to my neighborhood and open ethnic restaurants. It seems a new Thai restaurant opens every 15 seconds in Harvard Square. These great new foods keep life interesting and hopefully healthy.

- **soar.berkeley.edu/recipes/ethnic/chinese**
  Over 800 Chinese food recipes. Who knew bird nest soup had a real bird nest in it.
- **library.thinkquest.org/10320/Recipes.htm**
  Good "soul food" recipes and an interesting article on how they came about.
- **www.shango.net/cyberbride/sh.htm**
  Secret Russian recipes along with some sort of music which I guess could be Russian. It drives you crazy after awhile.
- **www.sas.upenn.edu/African_Studies/Cookbook/Ethiopia.html**
  Not only Ethiopian recipes but an article on how their meal is served.
- **www.al-bab.com/maroc/food/food.htm**
  Moroccan recipes enable you to enjoy some of the world's greatest cuisine.
- **www.latinsynergy.org/tm6.htm**
  A really large number of Latin American recipes sorted by countries, and links to even more.
- **soar.berkeley.edu/recipes/ethnic/indonesian**
  A total of 113 Indonesian recipes and I hope you read the section on indigestion first.

Some Fun Foods

- **4bagels.4anything.com**
  What is a bagel and what is its history. This site has this kind of interesting information along with shops and franchises should you want to go into the business.

- **www.gourmetgarlicgardens.com**
  How to grow garlic, its health benefits, all the varieties and probably vastly more than you'd ever want to know about garlic.

- **www.matkurja.com/slo/country/food/gobe**
  How to find and prepare wild mushrooms without dying which seems a goodly thing to learn.

- **www.dzpickles.com**
  Make your own pickles and sauerkraut with the kits this company sells.

- **www.fritolay.com/pretzel.html**
  The history and story of the pretzel.

Once I realized there were sites on bagels and pickles and garlic I just had to include them, though I don't know what they really have to do with being 40.

Chocolate

Mmmmmm. Now that we no longer "break out" when eating chocolate we can indulge our passion whenever we like or at least whenever we need a reward for a 10 mile bike ride or particularly tough aerobic class. You don't still "break out" do you?

- **www.hersheys.com/cookbook/chocolate/ideas**
  Lots of chocolate recipe ideas. If you open this site your diet is going to go to hell.
- **www.globalgourmet.com/food/ilc**
  Global Gourmet's I Love Chocolate site with mouth watering finds and recipes for each month as well as an archive that will keep you well supplied with chocolate ideas.
- **www.godiva.com/recipes/terms.asp**
  A good glossary of chocolate and baking terms as well as tips and more dessert and chocolate recipes than you could consume in a lifetime.
- **productopia.austin360.com/P/12/0,2557,12-451-0,FF.html**
  Life is too short to eat bad chocolate. This excellent site will teach you what to look for and give you buying advice.
- **www.exploratorium.edu/chocolate**
  The history of chocolate and factory tours explaining how it is made.
- **chocolate.scream.org**
  The chocolate lover's page with links to 774 chocolate sites around the world.

Gourmet Food Shopping

- **www.balducci.com/home.asp**
  Fancy and gourmet everything. You'll go broke just getting through the spice section. Much more fun than your regular supermarket.
- **www.onlygourmet.com**
  I had trouble getting past the chocolate section.
- **www.bighornbuffalo.com**
  You can eat Buffalo meat just like the Indians did. It has a lot less fat than beef which is why you never see a fat Indian in movies.
- **www.glutenfreemall.com**
  This site has combined the catalogs of many dietary food manufacturers to bring you 880 gluten free products.
- **www.shoppinghunt.com/sallycat.asp?CatID=300**
  Sally has links to every specialty food item you'll want and some you won't.

These sites are more fun than your regular supermarket. They are not only an easy way to shop but give you access to unusual special products and tastes and you had better be able to taste the difference cause they generally cost more.

Spices and Sauces

More places to find the endless specialties and varieties that make cooking and eating such fun. The mustards alone would fill all my kitchen cabinets.

- **www.mustardstore.com/default.htm**
  This is the world's biggest mustard store. If you tried to taste them all you'd burn your stomach out. There must be thousands.

- **www.chiletoday.com**
  Every kind of Chile and salsa along with recipes, tips and hot tamale news.

- **emall.com/spice**
  All the flavor secrets and spices of the orient. You'll never order take-out Chinese food again.

- **www.americanspice.com**
  Over 4,000 spices, oils, hot blends and other specialty supplies. If you can't find it here you don't want to put it in your stomach.

- **www.hothothot.com/hhh/index.shtml**
  The hottest of the hot including tastes like "Sure Death", "Cyanide" and "D.O.A.".

- **www.thewrath.com**
  Hot sauces and salsa from "Religious Experience" along with some entertaining recipes.

Dining Out Restaurant Guide

- **www.zagat.com**
  Zagat is the world's best restaurant review guide. It uses reader's ratings to rank the restaurants and I have seldom known it to be wrong. Unfortunately it covers only major cities.

- **www.food.com**
  Takeout or delivery from thousands of restaurants near your home.

- **www.restaurants.com**
  A list of restaurants in cities across the country and maps to help you find each.

- **www.fodors.com/ri.cgi**
  Fodor's expert restaurant reviews for restaurants in the cities they cover. You won't find every one listed but they tend to find the better places.

- **www.dinesite.com**
  Restaurants listed by location and broken down by cuisine and type. The ratings seemed to be very generous.

- **www.restaurantrow.com**
  Would you believe 100,000 restaurants listed in 24 countries. You could starve to death just deciding which to visit.

- **www.menusonline.com**
  A great restaurant guide for 16 major cities with menus, reviews, directions and even dress codes.

There are so many restaurants out there that it is comforting to have a few guides to help you pick out the good ones.

Beer

When we started drinking beer the taste was pretty much limited to the mild lagers that still make up the bulk of what's sold here. But recent years have spawned thousands of micro breweries with intriguing tastes and varieties that make choosing a beer a wonderful adventure. It's worth experimenting. If nothing more, your refrigerator will look more colorful. Don't let "experts" dictate what beer you should like and don't let descriptions of beer become as outlandish as those given to wine. Beer, after all still makes a 40 year old burp and pee.

www.breworld.com
Europe's large and excellent internet site for beer and brewing. Superb beer industry search engine plus hours of fun exploring breweries and ranking beers.

BeerMasters.com/BeerMasters
Beer Master's Tasting Society provide a superb glossary to help describe what you drink. Acetaldehyde, for example, is a green apple aroma produced as a by-product of brewing. I don't suppose you really need to know that to enjoy a beer.

www.siebel-institute.com/welcome
A school that teaches you to brew rather than just drink.

www.beerhunter.com
A splendid online magazine by Michael Jackson, the world's foremost beer journalist.

www.Heineken.nl
A history and a virtual tour of the Heineken brewery.

www.guinness.ie
The history of Guinness and lots of other fun information.

www.fostersbeer.com
You have to enter your birth date to see this site (hey, we're 40) but they do teach you to speak Australian.

www.pubcrawler.com/Template
A great site listing almost 4,000 micro breweries, more than you could sample in a lifetime, plus reviews and beer talk.

Wine

- **www.winespectator.com**
  The online version of Wine Spectator magazine. The wine basics are excellent for the unknowledgeable and will really teach you about wine.
- **www.drinkwine.com**
  This site has all sorts of information for the wine lover from food pairings to wine tours to growing your own.
- **www.vine2wine.com**
  A comprehensive wine site that connects you to everything. Sites like these could put authors like me out of business. In practice, however, even these good ones disappear.
- **www.wineculture.com**
  A hip wine guide to choosing, storing, buying, serving, and saving what's left.
- **www.wineenthusiastmag.com**
  The Wine Enthusiast magazine, rating and selling everything that has to do with wine.

At 40 some of us have graduated from the screw top caps and straw Chianti bottles that we used to stick candles in at college. Some may even have become wine snobs with different glasses for each variety of grape and a descriptive vocabulary of tastes that sounds like a botany textbook interspersed with a barrel makers inventory list. The sites shown here are for us 40 year olds in the middle who enjoy a good bottle of wine and haven't yet started annoying our friends with flowery descriptions.

Wine

I like reading wine reviews but I can never find any of the bottles reviewed when I go to a wine shop. I wonder if everyone has this problem. Don't let price influence your buying decisions. Expensive wines rarely come out on top in blind taste tests. Besides, anyone can find a great $100 bottle of wine. The skill comes in finding a great $10 bottle. Pick up a few terms from these wine sites and you can probably match wits with your friends who are wine experts.

www.tablewine.com
This site discusses affordable wines, around $10, with different topics each month.

www.wineauthority.com
Very authoritative and insightful wine reviews.

www.bandc.com
Reading this informative wine education site of over 200 pages will leave you sober enough to drive home.

www.stratsplace.com/wine.shtml
A superb site with thousands of the usual but also neat stuff like uses for corks, removing wine stains and printing wine tasting sheets.

www.thewinenews.com
This wine magazine reviews over a hundred wines each month and I particularly like the double blind tastings.

clifty.com/wine
A great wine tasting site run by regular folks like you and me and, in fact, here is a place where you can post your own ratings.

Wine and Beer Making

- **www.telusplanet.net/public/bhuisman/winetips.html**
  Good advice for learning to make your own wine.
- **www.hwbta.org**
  The Home Wine and Beer Trade Assoc. will teach you the basics and put you in touch with retailers who can sell you the equipment.
- **www.leeners.com**
  This well designed retailer's site shows you all the ingredients and equipment for making all kinds of booze as well as vinegar, cheese, mustard and soap. Hey, you can be self sufficient and go live in the woods.
- **www.beerbrew.com**
  Another fun site that will sell you all the equipment you need to try beer and wine making as well as providing instructions.
- **members.iquest.net/~ericg/ferment.html**
  This site tells you how to make simple fermented drinks and doesn't even try to sell you something. Sites like this are getting rare these days.

I think every 40 year old tries this at least once. I did. The beer wasn't too good but was fun to make. Then like most things you get interested in, something else comes along and now you have a bunch of bottles and stuff at the bottom of a closet.

Drink Recipes

Having a cabinet full of colorful and weirdly shaped bottles and a collection of mixing tools is almost as much fun as coming up with the concoctions. We used to call this our chemistry set.

- **www.bardrinks.com**
  Welcome to the party place. Drinks are categorized in many ways so you can find just the one you're looking for.

- **www.angelfire.com/mo/bartrick/bartrick.html**
  This is a fun site with bar tricks played with napkins, matches, glasses and things found around a bar. It also has drinking games, toasts, aphrodisiacs, recipes and more.

- **www.idrink.com**
  Just enter the ingredients you have around the house and this site will tell you what cocktails you can make. It sounds like there is a good party game here.

- **www.drinkboy.com**
  A nice alphabetic list of recipes for every drink you've ever heard of plus articles and discussion of bar tools.

- **www.inforamp.net/~mcdermot/drinks.html**
  An extensive list of readers' submissions of recipes. They range from "A Nother One Of Those" to "Zombie Piss".

Cigars

www.cigars.com
There are over 100 links here with every conceivable kind of information about cigars. Humidors, discount cigars, vintage cigars, and lots of cigar companies.

www.cigargroup.com
The Internet Cigar Group is an excellent site with some real solid information on all aspects of cigars. Their cigar brand database is very extensive.

www.cigaraficionado.com
This online version of Cigar Aficionado Magazine keeps you up to date with everything happening in the cigar world. Ratings of nearly 1,300 cigars.

www.cigarlife.com
An internet cigar magazine with daily news, monthly columns and feature articles. Their top 10 cigars each month is a fun section.

www.cigarfriendly.com
Cigar-friendly restaurants throughout the country as well as cigar reviews and events.

Cigars aren't quite as hot an item as they were a few years ago but still much more popular than before. One disadvantage of having cigars become a fad has been the prices. Popular and rare smokes have shot through the roof. On the other hand there's a lot more ratings and information and brands available and that does making smoking cigars more fun. There's no indoor place left, of course, where you can smoke them.

Hobbies, Pastimes and Interests

Hobbies may sound a little juvenile for a 40 year old but we all have these little collections and interests and I guess they qualify as hobbies for lack of a better word. And when dignified with the title "hobby" there is much less chance your mate will want to put the collection in the garage to make more space for their junk.

Photography

- **www.photography.com**
  A pleasant site with a good "Ask the Pro" section, photo news, search provisions and a daily contest.

- **www.onlinephotography.com**
  This site has some gorgeous photos and a well done, if limited, product review section.

- **www.kodak.com/US/en/nav/takingPics.shtml**
  Kodak's classic Guide To Better Pictures. This advice is so sound and so basic it makes you wonder why 95% of the photo-taking public ignores it. Worth reading and rereading.

- **www.bath.ac.uk/~masres/photo/manual.html**
  A good basic introduction to photography. Email this to your friends who are not good photographers and looking at their pictures will be much less painful.

- **home.netcom.com/~nikonman/phototips1.html**
  Very sound tips from a pro. This site is eminently readable and full of good ideas.

Everybody is a photographer and if everybody would just look at a few of these sites and learn how to really use their cameras we'd all be a lot less bored looking at everybody's boring pictures.

Gardening

This is a well covered subject on the internet and there are innumerable sites. I've just listed a few to help you get started but just type in "Gardening" and you'll be still reading while your garden withers away from lack of attention.

www.garden.org
The National Gardening Association has articles, tips and answers to your questions.

www.garden.com
A good place to buy 20,000 different products for your garden. Beautiful photos.

www.gardenweb.com
Lots of gardening resources are listed here with links to specialties such as Kitchen Gardens and Wildflowers. There are sections on seed exchanges and a botany glossary.

treeselect.com/treesearch.htm
Here is a great data base of trees categorized by color, shape size, growth rate and everything else you can think of.

garden-gate.prairienet.org
This has links to virtually every type of gardening web site imaginable.

www.sierra.com/sierrahome/gardening
Very inclusive site with plant encyclopedia, gardening software, timely hints and suggestions.

www.gardenguides.com
Guide Sheets on virtually every flower, herb, and vegetable with full color picture and detailed information on planting and care.

www.gardennet.com
"The premiere gateway to gardening on the net." With a plant and plant group information section, garden links, garden shop links, garden guidebook of public gardens by State, publications links, discussion area and books.

Flying

www.avhome.com/clubs-org.html
This site has a long list of flying and soaring clubs and of flying organizations. If you're new to flying, contacting a local club is a good way to start.

www.landings.com
A very comprehensive site with every weather link known, flight planning, pilot supplies, aircraft sales and hanger talk just to name a few.

www.faa.gov
Once again your government offers an excellent site with all sorts of FAA information. Regulations, pilot requirements, safety issues and so much more that only a government agency has the wherewithal to delve into.

www.homebuilt.org
There's no need to take up flying and spend a fortune buying an aircraft. With this site you can choose from dozens of designs and easily build your own plane. No thanks. I think I'll take the bus.

www.aeroseek.com/links/Images
Links to wonderful collections of fascinating aircraft pictures. This will fire you up to get a pilot's license.

www.aeroseek.com/links/Training_and_Education
This is the site that will teach you how to fly. Links to loads of schools and courses.

I've always wanted to fly and own a plane but every time I read about a private plane crash I get the willies. Do you think 40 is too old to learn to fly a helicopter? That's my real dream.

Coin Collecting

This is one hobby where you should make money if you don't do something stupid and buy just at the top of the market like my friend Ed did, jumping in when gold reached $800. Rare coins have historically increased in value and they're small enough to hide in an old shoe.

- **www.coinlink.com**
  You have just about everything here: auctions, books, coin grading, dealers and mints.
- **www.coinsite.com**
  A spectacular image gallery of rare coins plus answers to all your numismatic questions.
- **www.cybercoins.net**
  This online coin dealer has prices, descriptions and illustrations of expensive coins that they sell along with news and articles.
- **www.limunltd.com/numismatica**
  A great site with information about all phases of numismatic interests including news, frequently asked questions and a long list of splendid articles.
- **www.rare-coins.net**
  This site lists prices they'll pay for coins and currency. It's too bad the design is in gold on black cause you can barely read it.

Stamp Collecting

- **www.philatelic.com**
  An online mall for stamp collectors with many dealers, classifieds, a bulletin board and library.

- **www.usps.gov**
  The U.S. Post Office site with the latest stamps and stamp collectibles. It's good business for them. The profit's enormous when selling a stamp that doesn't get used.

- **www.philately.com/philately/index.htm**
  This site has a database, among much other information, of every country that ever issued a stamp and it's very long with some places I guarantee you've never heard of.

- **www.stamplink.com**
  This site claims to be the best in its category and it certainly seems to have links to the entire world of stamp collecting. I wouldn't start here unless it was a very rainy Sunday.

- **www.linns.com**
  This is the largest weekly stamp newspaper and besides keeping up-to-date you can search for zillions of stamps.

- **alfin.computerworks.net/index.html**
  A good beginner's introduction to stamp collecting and an easy site from which to get started.

The hobby of kings and presidents and anyone who may have to flee a country at a minute's notice and would like to take some of their ill-gotten gains with them. Just kidding. I'm sure most of my readers are honest hobbyists.

Antiques

Antiques are more than elegant collections that you hope will increase in value. They give you good excuses to travel and search and shop. If you specialize like you're supposed to, you could become an expert and uncover a real treasure every now and then.

- **www.curioscape.com**
  You can browse in over 500 categories of antiques and collectibles. Surely you'll find something of interest.

- **www.tias.com/stores/kovels**
  Kovels' on-line antique and collectible price guide with over 250,000 items in their database. Good information on how prices are established.

- **www.tias.com**
  You can browse for antiques by category. It's as much fun as wandering through shops where you'd have to search all day for the item you're interested in.

- **www.antiqnet.com**
  A good site to search for stuff in a long list of categories along with dealers and antique centers.

- **pages.ebay.com/antiques-index.html**
  You probably know about eBay and this is a brilliantly done antiquing place.

Collectibles

communities.msn.com/collectibles
News on what is becoming hot and what you should look for in the back of your garage.

www.mastercollector.com
A large doll and toy collector site.

www.collectiblesnet.com
All the toys, dolls, comics, glass and other junk that you threw out years ago is for sale here. Who kept all this stuff?

www.booksoncollectibles.com
Books on collectibles. Find out what your stuff is worth before taking it to the dump.

www.classic-cards-gifts.com
All the popular collectibles are here. The Bradford plates, Ty Beanies, Precious Moments etc.

acguide.kaleden.com
An extensive site of antiques and collectibles, shops, dealers, organizations, events and everything anyone ever thought of collecting.

This category overlaps of course with antiques, the terms being used casually for things others throw out that we want to keep for a while. Your next generation will throw it out. It's best to get involved with a fad early if you're interested in turning a profit. Buying Beanie Babies at the peak is only going to make someone else rich.

Astronomy

Think of how impressed everyone will be when you can name a constellation other than the Big Dipper. It also gets you out of the house if you're a cigar smoker or if the kids are playing loud music.

- **www.scopereviews.com**
  A great site about telescopes and superb advice for beginners.
- **www2.astronomy.com/astro**
  Astronomy Magazine's online site. I have always found the magazines about a hobby or sport are a good place to start when exploring a new interest. Read them first before running out and buying the equipment.
- **www.seds.org/galaxy**
  Some truly exciting pictures and a good guide to the solar system and space sciences.
- **www.mtwilson.edu/Services/StarMap**
  This site creates a free map of the sky customized for your locations and viewing time.
- **galaxy.tradewave.com/galaxy/Science/Astronomy.htm**
  This site indexes everything from extraterrestrial life to planetariums.
- **www.solarviews.com/eng**
  Magnificent views of the solar system. If this doesn't get you interested in astronomy nothing will.
- **www.seds.org/images**
  Space Images Archive with 13,000 breathtaking photos.

Birding

- **www.gorp.com/gorp/activity/birding.htm**
  A super birding site with species, regional guide, refuges, links and such.
- **www.npwrc.usgs.gov/resource/othrdata/chekbird/chekbird.htm**
  Bird checklists of the United States. Current information on bird distribution throughout the country.
- **www-stat.wharton.upenn.edu/~siler/birding.html**
  Birding on the net with a hot list for posting sightings, numerous links and the Sibley-Monroe classification.
- **www.birdfeeding.org**
  The National Bird-Feeding Society with bird feeding information unlike anything you've ever seen.
- **sunsite.sut.ac.jp/multimed/sounds/birds**
  An archive of bird songs.
- **www.nmnh.si.edu/BIRDNET**
  Links to more bird societies and resources than you'll be able to check out.

Birding is a lifelong quest which fits well into a 40 year old's scheme of things. Resist trying to set sighting records.

Family

Along with your health, the family is the most important part of your life so you might as well expand your knowledge of the relationships with the help of the internet. With luck you'll find a site that will help explain your kids, your mate and your pets. More likely you'll just end up more confused but you definitely will find lots of people in similar situations to chat with.

Parenting

- **www.family.go.com**
  One of those enormous all-inclusive sites that, if you really read it, would leave you no time to make kids, much less raise them. Lots for kids, from motivating them to study to craft activities.

- **www.parentsoup.com**
  Emphasizing baby years, it also carries you to the terrible teen period.

- **www.families.com/home**
  If you are dedicated to your children's learning, this site helps you discover if you have gifted children and gives you advice from playgrounds to books to colleges.

- **www.parenthoodweb.com**
  Expert advice on child care and parenting. By the way, all these sites have chat lines where you can commiserate with other parents whose kid-raising problems are probably worse than yours.

- **www.parenting-qa.com**
  Expert answers to your parenting questions. Just select a topic and find a pile of tips and advice.

- **www.mbnet.mb.ca/~ahawkins/frankchd.html**
  Twenty one wonderful "tricks" for taming children that should be copied out and reread and I hope this site is still there when you search for it.

You can never have too much expert advice on raising your kids especially when this expert advice changes each generation or so. To learn about the current theories, before they go out of style, tune into some of these sites.

Motherhood and Fatherhood

Learn about the job. It's taking up all your time so you might as well learn all you can and try to do a competent job. You will be graded on all this you know. Once the kids grow up they will give you a detailed critique.

- **www.thecybermom.com**
  A bit commercial looking but a delightful way to connect with other moms and all the things you are interested in.

- **www.cybermom.com/**
  A nice place for moms to meet and talk about kids, recipes, health, fitness and fun.

- **www.salon.com/mwt**
  A site for mothers who think and I think you'll like this place with its articles about family and things in general.

- **www.epinions.com/book-Family___Relationships-Motherhood**
  Good reviews on a load of books on motherhood.

- **www.fathermag.com**
  Fathering magazine has many articles on problems of custody and single parenting and a wonderful list of articles under "The Joy Of Fathering" section.

- **www.vix.com/pub/men/nofather/nodad.html**
  A library of articles on fatherhood and fatherlessness.

- **www.cyfc.umn.edu/Fathernet**
  FatherNet produces information on the importance of fatherhood, fathering and shows how fathers can be a good parent.

- **www.fatherhoodproject.org**
  This educational project develops ways to support men's involvement in child rearing. Lots of good links and reviews of books and videos.

Parties

www.party411.com/theme21.html
You may think theme parties are a dumb idea but this site at least starts with a "40 year old" party. What's wrong with that?

www.party-creations.com/birthday/index.htm
This company sells theme packages for parties and while you'll be able to get away with the kids' themes the adult ones are pretty dumb.

www.playpwr.com
This is for kids' parties. You should read her "Birthday Party Philosophy" which is excellent, but after that you have to pay for books.

rats2u.com/halloween/halloween_recipes.htm
If you are throwing a Halloween party you'll find absolutely everything on this site from recipes to clip art to skulls and make up.

www.geocities.com/~geiman
A load of party ideas and links to places to get music and decorations.

boardmanweb.com/party/party_themes.htm
Almost a hundred party themes for kids and adults with helpful links to carry them off.

There is no excuse anymore for having dull parties. You'll find lots of ideas here, and lots of companies selling you theme decorations, for both kid and adult parties.

Interacting With Your Kids - Theme Parks

They may not listen to you and they may be mortified over what you say when you drive them with their friends and are embarrassed by what you wear and think all your ideas are "prehistoric" but if you take them to a theme park they will be your best pal again. Here are a few.

- **www.screamscape.com**
  A theme park fan's personal guide and best touring tips to parks and attractions. Great reviews of rides.
- **members.aol.com/parklinks/links.htm**
  Absolutely total coverage of the entire theme park, carnival, state-county fairs, fun centers and ride world. They even have accident reports so you can work up your excuses for rides you'd rather skip.
- **www.geocities.com/~robbalvey**
  A couple's guide and ratings of theme parks and roller coasters. And, if you can stand it, 300 photos of their roller coaster honeymoon.
- **http://users.sgi.net/~rollocst/amuse.html**
  Links to every amusement, theme, water park and every other kind of fun center you can imagine.
- **themeparks.about.com/travel/themeparks**
  You can find every theme park, roller coaster, zoo and whatever in the world with this site.

Slang and Language

- **www.slanguage.com**
  American Slanguage guide that lets you pick a city and talk like the locals or look up the latest teen talk. Dat is crunk.
- **www.peevish.co.uk/slang**
  This site lets you plug in a word and find out its meaning. It's from the United Kingdom, where so much slang originated, so they should know.
- **www.miskatonic.org/slang.html**
  This claims to be a glossary of hardboiled slang but you'll actually recognize some of the terms. It's a long list and you'll enjoy becoming hip as you face this new language.
- **www.csupomona.edu/~jasanders/slang**
  College slang. You'll love the top 20 list. It has every word your kids use and you don't.
- **www.rapdict.org**
  This is a serious list of rap slang but I suspect it is out of date by the time it arrives on the internet.
- **dir.yahoo.com/Reference/Dictionaries/Slang**
  This site lists a load of slang dictionaries and if you get into them too deeply your own family will no longer understand you.

Are you having trouble understanding your kids? Do they use terms like peeps and warsh and yo sup that you have no idea of the meanings? The sites listed here will make you hip again so you can say all these hip things and sound like an idiot teenager whenever you want. Also, don't forget to put your hat on backwards.

Preparing For College

No, it's probably too late for you to sign up to get your MBA but it's not too soon to start saving for the kids' education. There are college sites listed that will give you an idea of costs and programs so you can stay knowledgeable about directions to guide your kids. They're not going to listen to you but if you beat them to the punch and have some ideas on schools and courses, with luck, you can nudge them the right way.

www.review.com
This site of the Princeton Review has everything you'll need to know about getting into any college. They even have a separate place for parents to click on.

moneycentral.msn.com/family/home.asp
Tips on saving for college, selecting a college and paying for college. What else do you need to know?

www.embark.com
Find, the right school for your kids. You can search out any college and even apply to leading colleges online.

www.usnews.com/usnews/edu/college/corank.htm
The U.S. News and World Report's annual college rankings. Find out if your old school still makes the grade.

www.universities.com
A data base of 3,000 colleges and universities broken down in many ways and with financial aid information.

www.collegeview.com
Virtual tours of hundreds of colleges. It sure beats driving all over the countryside.

Kids' Camps and Trips

www.camp.ca

Just type in the kind of camp you think your offspring would be interested in, whether it's sailing, riding, computer, cheerleading, gymnastics, foreign or weight loss and so many names will come up that you'll never be able to interview them all. It's unbelievable but there is a camp for every interest.

www.kidscamps.com

Another directory of camps that offers so many choices your kids will be fighting to go.

www.summercamp.org

This free public service will give you guidance and referrals for camps worldwide.

www.outwardbound.com

Teenagers should get excited about these adventure trips. In fact I got pretty excited and they take parents on some.

www.nols.edu

National Outdoor Leadership School offers superb leadership and outdoor skill courses in exciting wilderness areas.

If you are interested in a relaxing vacation by yourself you are going to have to find someone to leave the kids with or find a camp or trip of their own. The sites listed here will give you ideas for hundreds of exciting places to send kids which will educate them, broaden their horizons, expand their interests and leave you guilt free to take your own vacation.

Dogs

There should be someone in the family that you can really count on and if you take care of the feeding, your dog is going to be the one. He may protect the house and play with the kids and go to the vet with your mate but if you feed old Fido you are the one who'll get licked each night when you come home.

- **www.petnet.com.au/selectapet/dogselectapet.html**
  Select a dog that matches you and your life style at this site.

- **www.petnet.com.au/dogs/dogbreedindex.htm**
  Photos and descriptions of most every breed to let you see if you're going to like the dog the computer picked for you.

- **www.bulldog.org/dogs**
  Doggy information on the web. Links to specific breeds and all sorts of other information. My God they even cover wolves.

- **dogs.about.com/pets/dogs**
  Everything you need to know to care for your dog: grooming, health, housebreaking, food, training, shows plus lots more.

- **www.petrix.com/dogint**
  This site ranks the intelligence and obedience of various breeds. Don't feel inadequate if your pet comes out in the lowest quarter.

- **www.akc.org**
  Lots of help from the American Kennel Club on selecting and buying a pure bred dog.

Cats

- **www.cfainc.org**
  The Cat Fanciers Association with information on caring for cats, breeds and colors and the largest registry of pedigreed cats.
- **www.katsation.com/felinewww**
  Worldwide feline links with shows, breeds, rescues, pictures and everything.
- **www.openhere.com/hac/pets/cats**
  A real web of cat links. One, for example, has about a billion names for cats.
- **www.fanciers.com**
  Cat care, breeds, shows, medicine and many, many links to cat shelters and help organizations.
- **www.best.com/~sirlou/cat.shtml**
  The history, genetic, gestation, evolution, species chart, information on choosing a cat and anything else you can think of about cats.

Cats are different. They're independent and clean and clever and once you are into them you'll want to fill your house with felines. You've got to resist this urge.

Good Stuff for 40 Year Olds to know

If mates, kids, or friends ask questions us grown up 40 year olds have to know all about whatever they are asking. We're supposed to be experts by dint of our age alone. These sites will give you enough information so you can bluff your way out of almost any question.

- **www.howstuffworks.com**
  The How Stuff Works site will make you seem like a genius. It tells you how everything works and your kids and woman will think you're absolutely wonderful.

- **www.britannica.com**
  The whole Encyclopedia Britannica. What more could you ask for as an information source. I wonder what ever happened to all those people who used to sell them door to door?

- **www.wackyuses.com**
  You'll impress everyone when you show them how Coca Cola® can clean a toilet bowl, you can shave with peanut butter, use Jello® to style your hair and Miracle Whip® to remove chewing gum or dead skin.

- **www.virtualflowers.com**
  Send virtual flowers, for free, to your wife, mom or girlfriend. They'll love it. I've been meaning to send them to my wife for months.

- **www.urbanlegends.com/index.html**
  Hundreds of all those crazy stories you've been hearing all your life like alligators living in sewers and cow tipping and Spanish Fly are investigated, and discussed and mostly debunked here.

Maps

- **www.mapquest.com**
  Not only maps of every place but a detailed visitor's guide for everything you'll need from hotels to theaters once you get there.

- **www.maps.expedia.com/OverView.asp**
  A great site that lays out a map giving you accurate directions between any two points in North America. See how it gets you home.

- **www.mapblast.com/mblast/index.mb**
  Free maps and driving directions to all points in the U.S.

- **geog.gmu.edu/projects/maps/cartogrefs.html**
  This cartography resource has links to almost 100 internet map sites.

- **oddens.geog.uu.nl/index.html**
  This site has links to almost 10,000 map resources. If you can't find it here you probably don't want to go there.

- **www.library.yale.edu/MapColl/online.html**
  A neat site showing pictures of Yale University's historical map collection for the period 1500 to 1900.

- **hum.amu.edu.pl/~zbzw/glob/glob1.htm**
  Several hundred great images of the globe with fantastic space views, maps of surface temperatures, glaciers, fires, winds, everything.

- **www.mapsonus.com**
  This great site will draw a map of any address you type in or plan you a route between any two points.

- **www.nationalatlas.gov**
  U.S. Geological Survey shows just how much fun you can have with your tax dollars. Play with maps of all the U.S.

- **terraserver.microsoft.com/default.asp**
  Amazing as it sounds this site allows you to zoom in from space and see an aerial view of your house.

There is no excuse for getting lost with all the free maps and directions that are available on the internet. You'll even be able to answer the kid's question, "are we there yet?"

Good Information Sources

Besides knowing all about mechanical things, you can impress people with knowing how to find zip codes and addresses, weather, traffic and the correct postage to put on a package to Finland. It's all here.

- **www.upsp.gov**
  The post office site with prices and rates. Find out what that airmail letter to Afghanistan should cost.
- **www.reversephonedirectory.com**
  Have a friend's phone number, but need their address? Use the Reverse Phone Directory. Also great if you have Call Identifier and want to know who called you while you were out.
- **www.usps.gov/ncsc/lookups/lookup_zip+4.html**
  Need someone's zip code? Just enter the address, and you'll come up with their zip code + 4 as well as their county.
- **www.smartraveler.com**
  Traffic updated frequently for major cities in the US, with links to city-related travel services.
- **www.govworks.com**
  This site offers a free service finding information or answering questions about any of your governmental needs.
- **www.isbister.com/worldtime**
  This site gives you the time at almost anyplace you can spell in the world. Don't wake up your friends in the Solomon Islands by calling them at 3AM.

Etiquette

You'll need these sites to back you up when your family refuses to behave like human beings. It's also nice to know which foods you can eat with your fingers and how to dress for formal weddings.

www.albion.com/netiquette/book/index.html
Who knew there were so many rules to using the internet? There is a lot to read on this "net etiquette" site but if you go through it all you won't be in danger of showing up as a clod.

www.cuisinenet.com/digest/custom/etiquette/manners_intro.shtml
American table manners are tougher than I thought but at least there is a section on what you can eat with your fingers.

hospice-cares.com/hands/library/pt_care/gfriend.html
Some excellent suggestions on bereavement etiquette.

homearts.com/depts/relat/07wedqf1.htm
Wedding etiquette is a complicated matter and this site begins to answer some typical questions. You can send your own questions by email.

www.webofculture.com/refs/gestures.html
Travel etiquette is a minefield and this site gives you tips on proper behavior from Austria to Turkey. Never, for example, show the sole of your shoe in Turkey, and be sure to keep your wrists on the table in Bulgaria.

www.ci.sat.tx.us/planning/handbook/index.htm
This extensive handbook explains the etiquette of dealing with disabled people.

Astrology

You may be almost positive that astrology is all bunk but, just in case, it's still nice to be able to check. Find out if this is an auspicious day to make major internet decisions.

- **horoscopes.astrology.com**
  Enjoy a daily dose of destiny. Lots more at this site than just your sign profile and fortunately they're usually general enough so they don't frighten you to death.

- **horoscopes4u.com**
  Five hundred links for each Zodiac sign. This site could keep you busy for awhile and if you check each you'd have to give up some other time-consuming activities like sleeping, eating and working.

- **www.astro-horoscopes.com/index1.html**
  Learn the language of Astrology and explore many frequently asked questions. A large and very comprehensive site.

- **www.astrola.com/astrolog.html**
  Learn what a true horoscope involves and why it gives incredibly accurate advice and forecasts.

- **www.ntic.qc.ca/~rloise/english.html**
  Tibetan and Chinese Astrology. Much is in French as well as English which gives it an elegant authentic air.

- **www.astroamerica.com**
  The Astrology Center of America offers a national clearing house for Astrology books. The list is very extensive and you won't be able to pronounce the names of most of the authors.

Adult Education

- **www.back2college.com**
  An adult and back-to-college site that will link you to online programs as well as colleges offering programs.
- **www.womensu.com**
  Women's U is a virtual learning community for women, with classes conducted over the telephone.
- **www.edupoint.com**
  A supersite for adult education allowing you to search 3,000 learning providers with hundreds of thousands of programs from all over the country.
- **www.pbs.org/als**
  PBS adult learning service which will help you find out about distance learning and locate courses for home study.
- **www.suite101.com/welcome.cfm/adult_education**
  A good general adult education site with discussions, advice links and information.
- **www.edu-marketing.com/AdultEd.htm**
  News on adult and distance learning which puts a degree in the reach of everyone, even 40 year old women.

If you really want that administrative position you can probably get the advanced degree that you need by using the internet. You'll find the time by squishing it in between watching TV and surfing the net.

Literature

These literature sites will let you catch up on all the great works you should have read when you were hanging out in bars instead. If you need a little incentive, start with the books that were once banned.

- **authorweb.dingir.org**
  This site features 500 authors and you can link directly to them and get reviews and ratings of some of their work.
- **www.promo.net/pg/list.html**
  Thousands of books can be downloaded for free from this site once you learn how to use the download connections. You probably won't have to buy another book for the rest of your life.
- **vos.ucsb.edu**
  An incredible resource for all the humanities. Links to every genre of literature as well as all the humanities. It is incredible to imagine one individual developing this site.
- **andromeda.rutgers.edu/~jlynch/syllabi.html**
  Syllabi and literature course materials that are available on the web. If you are interested in expanding your knowledge in a particular area, this is a great place to start.
- **englishlit.about.com/arts/englishlit**
  This is an English literature site but you can explore the classic literature of virtually every other language by clicking on the left hand bar.
- **www.randomhouse.com/books/bannedbooks**
  A very long list of books that were banned at one time or the other. A fascinating site and now you can read them all.

Online Book Clubs

- **bookchatter.com**
  Books, chosen by members and reviewed by message board, are discussed monthly. Easy to navigate reading and discussion schedule, discussion page, previous reading selections. Books rated from 5 - 1.
- **books.rpmdp.com**
  A current reading schedule of books with dates during which discussion takes place via a listserve. You may express your opinion and rate the book from 10 - 1. Complete listing of books read and rated for the past 5 years.
- **www.mindmills.net/booklovers**
  Discussion list information, author of the month, and a listserve to join their discussion group.
- **www.aande.com/bookclub**
  A&E Cable Station book club to discuss both classic and contemporary literature. You have to register, but it is free.
- **women.com/clubs/book.html**
  Women.com's book club. Join other bookworms for message board conversations on all sorts of book-related topics and more.

Perhaps you would like a bit of interaction and discussion with your reading. The internet lets you do it on your own schedule and with people whose opinions and ideas you share and you never have to bring the snacks.

Film and Video Reviews

Why go to lousy films and rent boring videos just cause your mate, kids or friends pick them. Get the real ratings and reviews at these sites and make your own decisions. I for one like pirate movies.

- **www.filmgeek.com**
  Very complete reviews of new film and video releases.
- **www.film.com**
  In-depth reviews of current films, and there are more than you can imagine, plus any video you can think of.
- **www.imdb.com**
  A data base of every film released since the beginning of the century. This may be the best movie and video site on the web. They even tell you how to sell your old videos. The top 250 are particularly interesting and it seems I missed most of them.
- **mrshowbiz.go.com**
  Another wonderful entertainment site with TV rating as well as films and videos.
- **www.movie-reviews.com**
  Excellent and easy to use film and video reviews with star ratings.
- **www.filmsite.org**
  The Greatest Films specializes in classics. Wonderful descriptions of their top 100.
- **www.reel.com**
  Good reviews of current films as well as videos and DVD's.
- **entertainment.msn.com/movies/movies.asp**
  Just type in your zip code and it will give you theaters and showtimes.
- **www.foreignfilms.com**
  This is the place to find great foreign films on video and DVD.
- **www.cinema-sites.com**
  Films and video reviews, data bases, fan pages, trivia, scripts, schools and so much more it'll take you all afternoon just to get through the index.

Politics

- **www.e-thepeople.com**
  No need to go to rallies and risk freezing or even being beaten by the authorities like in the 60's. With this site you can pick an issue right on line and enter your petition.
- **www.politicaljunkie.com**
  Everything political is on this site. Perspectives, facts and figures, people and organizations, newspapers, government, everything.
- **www.thenewrepublic.com**
  Washington insider news and thoughtful articles on politics and foreign affairs.
- **politics.slate.msn.com/politics**
  Top stories and politics from around the country.
- **www.politics1.com**
  Links to all the political parties, issues and debates. Links to all political news sources, state races and campaign consultants.
- **www.democracynet.org**
  A public interest site for election information. The site is nonpartisan and funded by foundations.

You better start paying attention to politics if only to make sure there'll be some cash left in Social Security when you retire. Make sure those liberals don't tax you out of your birthright and that the conservatives don't legislate away your rights.

Men's Magazines

Men's magazines have been around almost as long as printing. We're not old enough to remember the Police Gazette but I think it showed an occasional picture of some shapely young lady in her underwear and was a big hit in the barber shops of its day. Present day men's magazines show a lot more, of course, but there are also magazines on health and sports and other things. Parts of some are online for free and these lists may introduce you to a few you never heard about.

- **www.maximonline.com**
  Maxim has beer, travel, fitness and lots of girls and this site gives you a wonderful flavor of the magazine. It's really supposed to appeal to younger guys but if you don't tell anyone you can enjoy it too.
- **www.manhood.com.au**
  An excellent online Australian magazine with lots of manhood forums and advice.
- **www.uploaded.com**
  The online version of the very sexy British magazine Loaded. Don't enter here if you are offended by coarseness.
- **www.askmen.com**
  An online men's magazine with a wide range of subjects like women, love, bodybuilding and whatever. It's free.
- **www.mensjournal.com**
  A general interest men's magazine with emphasis on adventure, travel, fitness and sport.
- **www.playboy.com/magazine/current/english**
  Here is Playboy, the old classic, and you'd better hope your internet access can download photographs quickly.
- **www.manslife.com/texttoc.html**
  The complete contents of a man's life and what a lot of information that is.
- **penthouse.com**
  You don't have to actually subscribe and be embarrassed when the post person delivers each issue. Most of Penthouse is right here on the web.

Women's Magazines

- **www.allthatwomenwant.com**
  All That Women Want is a British online magazine with all the usual advice, recipes, parenting etc. but with a delightful English flavor.
- **www.ellemag.com**
  The online site for Elle, the women's fashion and lifestyle magazine.
- **www.betterhomesandgardens.com**
  Food, gardens, homes, health, travel and all the other favorites from the online version of this classic women's magazine.
- **www.lhj.com/index.shtml**
  The Ladies Home Journal, online with food and health and beauty and shopping.
- **www.womentodaymagazine.com**
  An online magazine called Women Today with many features for young women but also lots on beauty, lifestyle, money, health and things like that.
- **thehistorynet.com/WomensHistory**
  Women's History has articles about the contribution of women in medicine, education, labor, business, and communications. It's fascinating.
- **healthyliving.women.com/hl**
  A magazine that promotes a healthy, balanced life style.
- **goodhousekeeping.women.com/gh/index.htm**
  Good Housekeeping Magazine gives you online advice on buying smart, eating and staying well, reviews of lots of different products and all the usual.

You probably know most of these magazines and have subscribed from time to time but now you can get much of the content for absolutely no cost. Whatever are they thinking as they give them away for free?

Weather

Remember how old people were always worrying about the weather? When people move to Florida they still delight in telling you just how cold it was last night in New England or wherever else you live. The advent of "wind chill" thrills anyone who lives in a warm climate and has relatives in the cold and a telephone with which to reach them.

- **www.accuweather.com/weatherf/index_corp**
  It's fun to enlarge and animate the map.
- **www.weather24.com**
  Weather24 will send the forecast to your email address so you'll always have the latest info.
- **www.cnn.com/WEATHER**
  If you want the weather in Japanese or Portugese you can get that also.
- **www.intellicast.com**
  Weather and forecasts anyplace in the world.
- **iwin.nws.noaa.gov/iwin/graphicsversion/rbigmain.html**
  The most complete, statistic laden, boring and hard to understand site, courtesy of your National Weather Service.
- **www.weather.com**
  Just fill in the zip code and up comes the weather. World weather as well and moving satellite pictures.
- **weather.yahoo.com/index.html**
  Current weather and 4 day forecasts. Weather maps, worldwide weather, ski reports etc.
- **www.washingtonpost.com/wp-srv/weather/historical/historical.htm**
  Historical weather for over 2,000 cities. Record highs, lows, rain, clouds, snow and everything else you can think of.
- **www.ncdc.noaa.gov/extremes.html**
  U.S. weather extremes and global historical records like 523 inches of rain in Columbia and 136 degrees in Libya.

Music For 40 Year Olds

- **www.oldiesmusic.com**
  On this site you can search oldies music of the 60's, and 70's. This is the good stuff that you can dance to, sing to and fall in love with.
- **www.on-air.com**
  An internet-only radio station where you can hear all your old favorites.
- **www.srv.net/~roxtar/oldies.html**
  Reviews of songs and artists from your formative years. You'll enjoy seeing the old names.
- **www.allmusic.com**
  An incredibly comprehensive source of music information. Thousands of reviews and audio samples, and you can search for anything in 6 languages.
- **www.stagebill.com**
  An excellent guide to the performing arts across the country: opera, jazz, dance, theater, classical. Just type in your city and what you'd like to hear.
- **www.geocities.com/SunsetStrip/Alley/4795/links.htm**
  Over 100 links to find The Beatles, ABBA, Simon and Garfunkle, The Rolling Stones and everyone else.

You've probably learned by now that "your" music isn't "their" music. Young people laugh at your taste in music but they are probably already too deaf to realize how great it is. Listed here are some place you can find just what you like.

Art

The richest most powerful kings of olden days couldn't have the art available that you do with a few clicks on your machine. Enjoy it.

www.artchive.com
An archive of over 2,000 works of art from over 200 artists with commentaries and galleries. The scans are excellent and you don't have to worry about crowds at your local museum.

www.wwar.com
A worldwide art resource that allows you to search galleries, artists, museums etc. There are for example 945 museums in the U.S. alone which should keep you busy for a few weekends.

www.artresources.com
Articles, reviews and guides to shows, museums and galleries plus over 2,000 images in their catalog.

www.art.com
Extensive art and poster collection searchable by artist, subject or color.

www.artcyclopedia.com
Browse by name or other searches to find any artist. Their top 30 artists, based on web popularity, is fascinating.

www.artlex.com
A visual arts dictionary of art-related terms that will allow you to hold your own at a cocktail party made up entirely of art historians.

witcombe.sbc.edu/ARTHLinks.html
A truly overwhelming site that categorizes and breaks down art by period, style and country and has incredible detail on each.

www.artmuseum.net
Almost as much fun as a trip to a great museum. This Intel sponsored site offers excellent quality tours of major exhibits.

www.art.net
Wandering through this site is like visiting the world's largest art colony as artists share their work with you. Sculptors, painters, digital artists and every other kind are all represented.

Dance

- **www.danceonline.com**
  Contemporary dance news, information, talk reviews and photos.
- **www.dancer.com/dance-links**
  All the dance links you could ever need. Ballet, modern, schools, newsgroups, performances, dancers, tap, flamenco, everything.
- **www.dancemagazine.com**
  Dance Magazine will keep you up-to-date on everything that's happening, who's doing what, with an extensive calendar.

Your ballet and tap dance days may be over but it's nice to keep up with the performances and people. Here is all the information.

- **www.artswire.org/Artswire/www/dance/browse.html**
  Another master list of seemingly every dance link in the universe. If you can't find it here you don't want to know about it.
- **www.webcom.com/shownet/kirov/ballink.html**
  This is the site where I found all the other master links. It gives about 50 links and you'll be too stiff to dance by the time you check them all.

Find Your Old Friends

There are lots of people finding facilities on the internet and it's a hoot to look up old friends. Find that bully from the sixth grade or your old high school flame.

- **www.infospace.com**
  Just type in the last and first name and, by God, they usually come up. You can also search public records to find out if they still owe you money.
- **www.theultimates.com**
  This site searches by several engines and if you use it a lot will give more features and better service for 12 bucks a year.
- **www.knowx.com/free/peoplefinder.htm**
  This ultimate people finder uses real estate and change of address records as well as phone books to find the long lost ones.
- **www.worldemail.com**
  A world email directory with 18 million listings in 6 different languages.
- **www.reunion.com**
  An online missing persons bulletin board and registry. Maybe someone out there is looking for you.
- **www.search-shark.com**
  A serious people searcher that uses military records, Social Security numbers, death notices and public records as well as the usual.

Genealogy

Find out if there are any nobles among your ancestors and if there is a castle or crown waiting for you in Slobania.

- **www.cyndislist.com**
  The most spectacular genealogy site on the web. Your one stop spot for more than 63,000 links most of which are categorized and cross-referenced in over 120 categories, such as country or religion. Constantly updated.

- **www.familysearch.org/sg/DisTree.html**
  This Mormon site is an excellent source of genealogical records. It's a good way to begin your search with information on methods, addresses of sources, and untold helpful hints.

- **www.ancestry.com/search/main.htm**
  Constantly updated database of over 500 million names. The information is only available to those who join at a fee, but, if you're intent on tracing your family, this is the place to go.

- **www.oz.net/~markhow/ukbegin.htm**
  Beginning genealogic research for England and Wales. Links to civil registrations, census returns, parish registers, books and other internet links.

- **www.jewishgen.org**
  Primary internet source connecting researchers of Jewish genealogy worldwide. Contains a database of over 175,000 surnames and towns, Shtetl Links for over 200 communities, and a variety of databases.

- **www.polishroots.com/genpoland/index.htm**
  If your family came from Poland, this is an excellent place to begin research into your family's history.

- **www.geocities.com/SiliconValley/Haven/1538/germ_rus.html**
  List of German-Russian Genealogy Links.

- **www.irish-insight.com/a2z-genealogy**
  Over three hundred Links to genealogy of Ireland and Northern Ireland.

a

b

c

d

e

f

g

h - i

OTHER GREAT BOOKS BY BOSTON AMERICA

The fine cultivated stores carrying our books really get ticked if you buy direct from the publisher so, if you can, please patronize your local store and let them make a buck. If, however, the fools don't carry a particular title, you can order them from us for $8 postpaid (unless otherwise noted). Credit cards accepted for orders of 3 or more books.

#2700 Rules For Sex On Your Wedding Night
All the rules from undressing the bride to ensuring the groom will respect her in the morning.

#2704 What Every Woman Can Learn From Her Cat You'll learn that an unmade bed is fluffier and there's no problem that can't be helped by a nap among many others.

#2706 Is There Sex After 50?
Everything from swapping for two-25-year olds to finding out it's not sexy tucking your T-shirt into your underpants.

#2707 Beer Is Better Than Women Because...
Beers don't change their minds once you take off their tops and don't expect an hour of foreplay.

#2708 You Know You're Over 30 When...
You start wearing underwear almost all of the time and no longer have to lie on your resume.

#2709 You Know You're Over 40 When...
You feel like the morning after and you can swear you haven't been anywhere and you start to look forward to dull evenings at home.

#2710 You Know You're Over 50 When...
Your arms aren't long enough to hold your reading material and you sit down to put on your underwear.

#2713 Unspeakable Farts
These are the ones that were only whispered about in locker rooms like the "Hold Your Breath Fart" and "The Morning Fart".

#2714 101 Great Drinking Games
A remarkable collection of fun and creative drinking games including all the old favorites and many new ones you can barely imagine.

#2715 How To Have Sex On Your Birthday
Finding a partner, the birthday orgasm, birthday sex games and much more.

#2717 Women Over 40 Are Better Because...
They are smart enough to hire someone to do the cleaning and men at the office actually solicit their advice.

#2718 Women Over 50 Are Better Because...
They don't fall to pieces if you see them without their makeup and are no longer very concerned about being "with it".

#2719 Is There Sex After 40?
Great cartoons analyzing this important subject from sexy cardigans to the bulge that used to be in his trousers.

#2721 Cucumbers Are Better Than Men Because...
They won't make a pass at your friends, don't care if you shave your legs and stay hard for a week.

#2722 Better An Old Fart Than A Young Shithead
A great comparison of the Old Fart who dresses for comfort and the Young Shithead who is afraid of looking like a dork.

#2726 Your New Baby
This is a manual that explains everything from unpacking your new baby to handling kids' plumbing and routine servicing.

#2729 Great Bachelor Parties
This book tells it all from finding a cooperative stripper to getting rid of the father-in-law to damage control with the bride to be.

#2730 Rules For Engaged Couples
Rules for living together, meeting the family, learning to share and planning the wedding.

#2731 The Bachelorette Party
Great pre-party and party ideas and suggestions for everything from limos to outfits to strippers to your behavior in bars.

#2732 Brides Guide To Sex And Marriage
Dealing with your husband's family and learning what he does in the bathroom and secrets of sleeping comfortably together.

#2501 Cowards Guide To Body Piercing
Cartoons and explanations of all the good and horrible places you can put holes in yourself.

Specially priced books:

#1500 Fish Tank Video [$15 postpaid] This fish tank video enables you to experience all the joys of beautiful, colorful and graceful tropical fish without having to care for them. You'll find yourself hypnotized by the delicate beauty of these fish. Approximately 1 hour running time.

#3001 Winning at Strip Poker [$14 postpaid with playing cards] Not only does this book give you tips on winning at poker, but it tells you how to talk beautiful women into playing with you and shows you what they should look like in 96 pages of full color. It also provides a deck of cards with extra aces to help you win.

#3002 Slightly Kinky Sex Games [$10 postpaid] The games include lots of ideas for oils and ice and places and tie ups and should keep a couple's sex life sizzling with imaginative new activities for a year. 96 pages of sexy full color pictures.

#3003 America's Greatest Hooters [$10 postpaid] 96 pages of full color photographs of America's best including the Louisiana Lollipops, New York Knockers, Georgia Peaches, Pennsylvania Pendulums, Minnesota Minis and lots of others.

NEW INTERNET BOOKS!

#2733 Bizarre Internet Sites [$8 postpaid]
Hundreds of unusual and wild internet sites that will shock, disgust and amuse you and take you places you never imagined even existed.

#3100 Kavet's Internet Sites for Your Wedding and Honeymoon [$10 postpaid]
This is a manual that explains everything from unpacking your new baby to handling kids' plumbing and routine servicing.

#3101 Kavet's Internet Sites for Men Over 50 [$10 postpaid] Fifty year olds need all the help they can get and this book gives them almost 1,000 internet sites.

#3102 Kavet's Internet Sites for Women Over 50 [$10 postpaid] This is a manual that explains everything from unpacking your new baby to handling kids' plumbing and routine servicing.

#3104 Kavet's Internet Sites for 40 Year Olds [$10 postpaid] When you are 40 you are busy with a job and kids and houses and cars. This book gives you almost 1,000 internet sites on these and subjects you'd like to make time for like travel, hobbies and sports.

BOSTON AMERICA C•O•R•P

125 Walnut Street, Watertown, MA 02472
tel: (617) 923.1111 • fax: (617) 923.8839